MEDIA MAGIC

Instantly Get Radio, TV, Print,
and Internet Press to Give
You Limitless Publicity

Created by
Conscious Living Publishing

For information contact:

Shannon Burnett & Associates, LLC
Conscious Living Publishing
PO Box 111333
Palm Bay, Florida 32911
321-549-2128

ConsciousLivingPublishing.com
ShannonBurnett.com
FreePressTraining.com

Participating Authors

KeithLeon.com
PaulaLangguthRyan.com
AmondaRose.com
AutomaticallyYou.com
BoldMarketingSolutions.com

ISBN: 978-0615962597

DISCLAIMER

All use of *MEDIA MAGIC - Instantly Get Radio, TV, Print, and Internet Press to Give You Limitless Publicity* is subject to the disclaimer below. Any use of such content constitutes the user's agreement to abide by the following terms and conditions:

What people are saying about *Media Magic*

"*Media Magic* details the entire process for getting your publicity everywhere for FREE!!" – **Dr. Joe Vitale, bestselling author of *The Attractor Factor* and featured in *The Secret***

"*Media Magic* brings a broad wealth of knowledge and experience to help any business looking to expand. It helped me develop a detailed plan, build a team, and execute multiple projects simultaneously."
— **Steve Crimi Sr., Electric Affect**

"Shannon is a very knowledgeable, fun, and experienced business person who has lots to offer to business owners and creative artists."
— **Veronica Panov, Attorney at Law**

"Shannon is a true pool of wisdom, and her method of teaching comes from such a place of sharing and passion that her messages are carried even deeper than you might expect. She has a gift for helping people recognize their value and what they have to offer, and provides a roadmap to taking your business and message into the world."
— **Renee Frechette, Qi Revolution**

"Best bang for my buck in a long time."
— **Carolyn, Franchise, Inc.**

"*Media Magic* will teach you how to get noticed, build credibility, and become irresistible to the media" – **Keith Leon, multiple bestselling author, publisher & mentor**

"The step by step strategic process not only helped me develop an amazing bio and press kit, but I relearned things about myself I had forgotten." – **Ben Winkler, 1988 Nobel Peace Prize recipient**

CONTENTS

ACKNOWLEDGEMENTS

This *Media Magic* book and project has taken me almost three years to complete and many people have encouraged and supported me during the entire process. There were many times when I thought we would never finish. However, with persistence and support, it is finally complete. I want to acknowledge everyone who participated for their help, because without them, this project would never have been finished.

This project started out as a basic tele-class for the exhibitors, sponsors, and speakers for my tradeshows. I wanted my business partners to be successful, profit from their investment, AND keep coming back year after year. I decided the best way to accomplish that, was to teach them to position themselves as experts in their chosen fields. As a result, my tradeshows also benefited from the Free Publicity they generated...WIN – WIN – WIN! These individuals and others saw the success and started asking me for deeper training and more tools – but I resisted for some time.

My friend, public speaking coach, and trainer, AmondaRose Igoe helped me make the shift to offering more training by helping me develop a power-packed day of Free Press training. She even drove over 3 hours to participate in my first public Free Press Bootcamp event! I am so grateful for her amazing skills and the work she has done – she has been an angel in my life. Thank you, AmondaRose, for always believing in me and helping me put my wisdom and experience in a format that has helped many people get their message out. We have seen hundreds of people go through my day-long training or one-on-one consulting and see immediate results! Thank you, too, for sharing "Hiring the Heavens," and for your coaching, which has made an impact on thousands of lives.

Special thanks to my 17+ year friend, Aaron Murakami, for his inspired idea to put this valuable material into a workbook that can reach many more people. This man is a genius – inventor, consumer health advocate, and co-founder of the largest Energetic Forum. Thank you, Aaron, for your encouragement, patience, and feedback. This project would never have happened if you had not helped keep me focused and provided a system of success. Thank you for never giving up!!

Thanks too, to Janice Holden, my amazing rock. She is the "secret behind the sauce." Janice is one of the most talented women I know — artist, graphic designer, skilled copywriter, and editor. Her support helped me bring my vision to fruition as she did everything from copywriting to being a shoulder to sharing life's challenges. Thank you, Janice, for your continued support as a dear friend, and for being by my side through the many transformations of life. Thank you, too, for helping create the most amazing day of my life, my wedding on 11-11-11. PLEASE give special thanks and see her amazing work in Chapter 2's *Visualize Your Success*.

Special thanks to Nick Turriff for his endless support in life over the past 4 years. Nick is always my "get it done" man!! In addition to helping me with the production of the Free Press Bootcamp "LIVE" events, Nick has developed websites, press releases, and so much more.

Thank you to my teacher and mentor, Bernie Dohrmann of CEOSpace International, and to my entire family at CEOSpace. If you have a business and are serious about growing it, this organization has a 20+ year track record of collaboration and success.

Thanks to Paula Langguth Ryan - a legend in copywriting and so humble and generous with her compassionate mediation and prosperity coaching. Thank you for teaching me to say YES to the universe and for always being willing to come play!

I have a deep appreciation for Rob Wilson of Cowboy Wisdom. His words and message continue to expand my mind and consciousness.

I am so grateful to Spirit for teaching me tools like muscle testing, "ask and you shall receive," offering help to others, and guiding me to the right people at the right time to create win-win-win experiences.

Special thanks to all my clients who have implemented these strategies, and proven that they really work! Your encouragement and enthusiasm are greatly appreciated.

Thank you to all of the authors who have joined forces *in Media Magic* to help everyone become more successful. I, myself, have learned and used so much valuable information and so many useful tools from working with them. They all brought amazing insight and wisdom to this project.

I am forever grateful for my mentor, coach, and dear friend Keith Leon of Babypie Publishing known as "The Book Guy." He has shared a number of publishing strategies and even secrets that saved both time and money with this project and many others in the near future.

Endless thanks to my family, for their continued support and unconditional love. My wonderful mother–in-law has spent countless hours helping with edit and ideas. Special thank you to my husband, Ari, and my beautiful and amazing children, Alex, Makayla, and Ryan. You keep me grounded and show me what it really means to live life to the fullest!

Partners in Health and Success,
Shannon Burnett-Gronich
Event Production Goddess,
Marketing Expert, and
Best Selling Author
(321) 549-2128 Office
ShannonBurnett.com
FreePressTraining.com
ConsciousLivingSpace.com
ConsciousLivingPublishing.com

Spend 7 adventurous days exploring volcanoes, swimming with dolphins, sacred sites, and your amazing self in Hawaii. "Join us on this Dare to Live Challenge and experience the heart-pumping exhilaration of this life-changing event!"
It doesn't get much better than this!   DaretoLiveChallenge.com

INTRODUCTION

"Marketing is the key to building a successful business. Without it, you have no business being in business"
— Shannon M. Burnett-Gronich

Imagine with me for a moment that you are sitting at your dining room table having breakfast, and you pick up your morning newspaper. When you open it, you see your top competitor on the front page with a huge photo, showcasing their business. You are surprised and think, "Wow, how did they manage to do that?"

Then you get up from breakfast and you go turn on the television to catch up on the local news and there they are again being interviewed by a T.V. anchor. You *gasp* with disbelief. How could this be? You say to yourself, "Why aren't I getting this kind of attention?"

You decide to go for a drive and clear your head. As you are taking a nice relaxing drive, you are listening to your local radio station. All of a sudden, you hear the name of that company again and they are being called the "Best in Town!" You have had enough. It is time for you to get extreme results. It is time you get your message to the world now.

Ladies and Gentlemen, you are in the right place. This program will help you learn the simple step-by-step process to take your message to the masses *now*.

Thank you for being proactive in your business and your commitment to spread your message to the world. I have put my heart and soul into my *Media Magic*, and I am committed to doing whatever it takes to be certain your time and investment was well spent.

SUCCESS STRATEGIES

Media Magic

SUCCESS STRATEGY
1
Why *Media Magic*?

*"One of the greatest pieces of economic wisdom is to
know what you do not know"*
– John Kenneth Gilbraith

Before we get started, I would like to tell you a little bit about myself.
Most people think that marketing and press releases are something
that comes natural to me. How many of you think that is true?

As a single mother of two kids, my financial situation was always a
struggle. It seemed like no matter how hard I worked, with daycare
and the cost of living, at the end of the day I was still broke.

I had a profound moment in my life that inspired me to start a
business to help others find solutions for their health challenges. I
didn't know how to start a business or run a business, let alone *grow*
a business. Talk about being scared! I knew that in order for ANY
business to be successful, it must market itself to get customers.
How would I reach MY market with no money to work with??
Successful marketing always costs money... or so I thought!

At that point, I started to really look at the concept of marketing.

What is marketing? How much does it cost? What makes a
companies marketing successful? I didn't learn this in school. I
committed myself to learning everything I could about marketing
because I knew if my business was going to succeed, then getting
free press was my only way. I started to look at businesses that had
articles published in the newspaper and business people who had
been interviewed on the radio. I started studying ways to get free
publicity.

Then I ran into my first mentor, Paul Hartunian. Paul knew the secrets and brought in over a million dollars in free press - selling the Brooklyn Bridge! I started applying his strategies and got over $25K in free press for my first event. I was blown away by the results! Using the secrets I had learned, I took the same event from 800 attendees to *over* 2000 the next year, with over $75,000 in free press. I started seeing a simple system that *anyone* could use to expand any marketing budget and get free press.

Do you have a message you feel so passionate about that you have to get it out there?

Do you want to grow your business to the level of success you thought you could only dream about?

If you answered "Yes" to either question, my *Media Magic* workbook is your easy "How To" guide to getting your message out there and growing your business to extraordinary heights. This is the reason why you have purchased this training program.

In *Media Magic*, you will learn some of the most valuable information available that will help you grow your business and share your message. Through visualization, you will get a clear picture of who you are and where you want to be. You will develop a marketing plan specific to your business and learn how to tell your story in print and in short introductory speeches. As we progress through the program, you will learn why it's important to share your message in terms of benefits, rather than features. We will review the importance of press kits, and you will create your own complete press kit focused on two key ingredients: the power bio and press releases. And finally, you will learn how to get your message to the media, from initial contacts to critical follow-up.

How many of you would agree that we tend to make things harder than they are? I am going to break the whole *Media Magic* process down to simple, easy steps that you can duplicate on your own. I am going to share all of the mistakes I have made with you so you can save time and money by *not* repeating them. If you are committed to letting go of the concept that this is hard, I want you to follow each Success Strategy section and activity in this book by saying **"That's Easy!"**

"People often say motivation doesn't last. Well, neither does bathing, that is why we recommend it daily"

-Zig Ziglar

SUCCESS STRATEGY
2
Visualize Your Future

"You must see your goals clearly and specifically before you can set out for them. Hold them in your mind until they become second nature"
— Les Brown

Many people do not take the time to visualize what their successful business looks like and how they can create that success through marketing opportunities. Before you can develop a truly successful marketing plan, you have to know what you want your business to look like. Visualization tools will help you better understand what you want and how you will get there.

ACTION STEP 1: *VISUALIZE YOUR SUCCESS*

CREATE A VISION BOARD

A vision board is a great tool that will help you 'see' exactly what you want in your business and your personal life. Simply put, a vision board is a collection of images that helps you visualize the things you want to manifest in your life. It serves as a constant visual reminder of what you hope to achieve. There are several software programs and websites available that can help you with your board, but we recommend that you create your board "offline" for best results. Here are a few tips to help you as you create your business vision board:

1. Select the background for your board. You can use a cork board, a scrapbook, or a poster board collage. While all of these options have benefits, we recommend a cork board, so that you can change the images from time to time to keep your vision current. This is easier to do if you are using a cork board and push pins to create your vision board.

2. Focus this board on your business vision. You can create other boards with more personal themes, but it's a good idea to keep them separate and streamlined.

3. Take a few minutes to think about what you really want for your business before you start working on your board. Let yourself imagine the PERFECT situation, without limitation.

4. Find your images. It is important that your images reflect a clear picture of how you see your business and your role. Your vision board should make you feel excited about your potential and confident about where you are going.

   a. Look through printed material - magazines, newspapers, brochures, etc. - and cut out images that clearly reflect your vision. Go online to search and print images and phrases. Collect more than you need, and don't try to filter your selection yet! It's better to have too many and whittle down your collection than to pass something by and later wish you'd saved it.
   b. Take your own photos to add to your vision board. An office building that represents your 'dream' location, furniture, and equipment - anything that will help build your vision.
   c. Think of a magazine or newspaper you would like to be in and re-create an article from that publication with your picture in it. For example, if your vision is to become a top chef, create an article about or by you for Bon Appetit® magazine - maybe even a cover!
   d. Words are powerful, and adding some well-chosen words and phrases to your board will increase the power of the images. Select words and phrases that support your business vision, and how you see yourself in it.

5. Once you have a good collection of images and phrases, start putting your vision board together using the very best pieces from your collection. Save those that you don't use in a file or envelope in case you decide you want to use them later.

6. Place your vision board somewhere prominent, so that you will see it often throughout the day. You may want to take a photo of your board to keep in your purse or briefcase if you are frequently away from your original. Another option is to make another version in a small notebook. The more often you see your vision board, the more effective it will be.

7. Spend a few minutes each day looking at your vision board and thinking about each image. SEE yourself in each picture, feel the positive changes, read the words and phrases and 'breathe' them in. Imagine how your life will change and what you will be doing, saying, and thinking.

8. It is very important that you get a strong, positive feeling from your vision board. Update your board images and phrases frequently to be sure your board is a crystal-clear reflection of your vision. Frequent changes will prevent your vision board from getting stale - just be sure that your new images effectively represent your vision.

Media Magic

SUCCESS STRATEGY
3
What Is Marketing?

"Many a small thing has been made large by the right kind of advertising." – Mark Twain

"That's your big marketing plan?"

There are *hundreds* of ways to market yourself. The KEY to maximizing your marketing dollars is to identify the marketing tools that best suit your business by understanding the impact they can have on your business and utilizing as many suitable means as possible.

ACTION STEP 2: *DEVELOP YOUR MARKETING PLAN*

Take a few minutes and think of the many ways you might market your business. Brainstorm by writing all of your ideas down. Don't try to analyze or criticize your ideas at this time. The point of brainstorming is to come up with as many ideas as you can as quickly as you can.

_____

_____

_____

_____

_____

_____

_____

_____

_____

Now that you have come up with your list, let's take a look at some essential marketing tools AND some other great marketing options.

"Without strategy, content is just stuff, and the world has enough stuff."
– Unknown

Essential marketing tools that every business must have are:

Business Cards
Website
Brochures
Name Tags

Other means of marketing include:

- Social Networking
- Postcards
- Billboards
- Radio
- TV
- YouTube
- Articles
- Joint Ventures
- Licensing
- Signage
- Vehicle Wraps
- Direct Mail
- Blogs
- Email Signature
- Press
- Radio
- Presentations
- Word of Mouth
- Networking
- Classes
- Billboards
- Benches
- Flyers
- Telemarketing
- Tradeshows
- Conferences
- Public Speaking
- Internet
- Web Advertising
- Promotional Items
- Affiliate
- Opt-ins
- Magnetic Signs
- Email Blasts
- Auctions
- Testimonials
- Sponsorship
- T-Shirts
- Writing Articles
- Print Advertisements
- Blimp or Plane Banner
- Tele-class
- Webinar

Which of your marketing ideas did you see on my lists of marketing essentials and options?

_____

_____

_____

_____

List any ideas you came up with that did NOT show up on my lists of marketing essentials and options:

Now list ten marketing ideas that you would like to use to build your business:

1. _____

2. _____

3. _____

4. _____

5. _____

6. _____

7. _____

8. _____

9. _____

10. _____

That's Easy!

SUCCESS STRATEGY
4
What's Your Story?

"The basic building block of good communications is the feeling that every human being is unique and of value."
– Unknown

There are 3 types of stories that get publicity over and over again.

Human Interest
Community Events
Education

The more you can include all three, the more success you will have getting free publicity!!

ACTION STEP 3: *WRITE THREE (3) STORIES ABOUT YOU OR EVENTS THAT HAVE OCCURRED IN YOUR LIFE.*

What's your story (what has made you the person you are today)?

_____
_____
_____
_____
_____
_____
_____

What is an adversity you have overcome?

_____
_____
_____
_____
_____
_____
_____

How have you helped or inspired others?

_____
_____
_____
_____
_____
_____
_____

Story 1:

_____
_____
_____
_____
_____
_____

Story 2:

_____

_____

_____

_____

_____

_____

_____

_____

_____

Story 3:

_____

_____

_____

_____

_____

_____

_____

_____

_____

When creating your stories, remember to include
Who, What, When, Where, Why, and How.

That's Easy!

Media Magic

SUCCESS STRATEGY
5
Know Who You Are!

"There is always someone who can benefit from knowledge you are willing to share." – Unknown

When you start contacting the media, it is important to communicate your message clearly and concisely. You want to be sure that you are very clear about who you are and what your business is about. Don't give too much information - you may overwhelm them and "turn off" the contact! You might say, "I know who I am." But the key is to be able to explain it to others in a compelling way. Have you ever met someone at a networking meeting and they tell you what they are doing and after 10 minutes of explaining, you don't have a CLUE what they do? Can you clearly explain what your business is doing in a way that is interesting, innovative, and unique?

It is so important to be able to get your message across quickly, concisely, and in a compelling manner. Imagine that you have just stepped into an elevator with the ONE person you know can really help you and your business succeed.... Oprah, Donald Trump, Steven Spielberg.... you get the idea. You have only 30 seconds to get your message across before you reach the next floor. What would you say?

These short-form, complete introductions are often referred to as "Elevator Speeches," because they should take no longer than the amount of time it takes to ride a few floors with someone. An even better name might be "Conscious Calling," as your introduction should truly represent you and the passionate message you have to share.

Avoid saying "www" when sharing your website name. If time is of the essence and/or you are on the radio, every second counts. I recommend that each of us be prepared with a 15-second, 30-second, and one minute elevator speech. If you have an opportunity to share your message with someone in person or on the radio, you want to be prepared to use every single second WITHOUT going over or getting cut off in the middle!

There are a few key things to remember when creating your Conscious Calling:

- **SEE IT** Visualize a problem you and your business can solve, or a scenario that will get people engaged

- **WHAT'S SO GOOD ABOUT THAT?** In other words, share in the form of benefits. Don't just tell people WHAT you do, tell them HOW it can help them or someone they know!
  (More on this in Success Strategy 6!)

- **K.I.S.S or "KEEP IT SHORT AND SIMPLE"**
- Be sure to communicate as if you were speaking to a 10-year old child, using words that a child would understand

So, let's get started!

ACTION STEP 4: PREPARE A 30-SECOND CONSCIOUS CALLING/ELEVATOR SPEECH/BUSINESS INTRODUCTION ON A 3X5 INDEX CARD.

Here are three examples of effective 30-second Conscious Callings:

SAMPLE ONE:

I am Shannon Burnett-Gronich. I have produced over 300 events, tradeshows, and conferences since 2001 with up to 100+ exhibitors and 100+ volunteers. I have discovered that most sponsors, speakers, and exhibitors do not have the plan or education to be successful. In order for them to continue to come back year after year, I developed a simple system to train businesses and their teams in the fine art of conference excellence - helping them get the results they want and make more money. I have also been an exhibitor of multiple booths that required planning, marketing, team training, sales, database building, and follow-up. I have the ability to systemize and implement a plan for follow-up so that all leads turn into cash through investors, joint venture partners, product sales, and sponsors.

My event production clients include Dr Linda Hole, Jim Self, Stewart Levine, Esq. of Resolution Works, Dr. Gary Null – America's #1 Health Guru, and T Harv Eker – Secret to the Millionaire Mind.

If you or someone you know wants to turn their booth or event into a successful money-making experience, let me know or go to ShannonBurnett.com.

SAMPLE TWO:

I am Shannon Burnett-Gronich - speaker, coach, and Amazon #1 Best Selling Author of The Law of Business Attraction co-authored with T. Harv Eker of the Millionaire Mind.

I have personally trained and coached hundreds of individuals and businesses in all areas of their life - Marketing, Business Development, and Personal Growth. I'm passionate about helping others succeed through my global network.

I am blessed to have created an exclusive "Million Dollar Rolodex" and I possess a unique ability to teach others how to do the same. My clients go from wishing and hoping for the success they desire to actually achieving their business and personal goals in record time!

If you or someone you know is ready to take their business and their life to another level today, let me know or go to my website ShannonBurnett.com.

SAMPLE THREE:

Let me share three key things about publicity you may not be aware of. Free media is REALLY free. Someone speaking about you has more impact than you. Thousands of dollars in media have your name on them, right now! My name is Shannon Gronich, I am an Amazon bestselling author that has successfully attained over $3.1 million dollars in free publicity and want to teach you how to do the same.

If you or someone you know wants to position themselves at the top of their industry, contact me at info@FreePressTraining.com or go to FreePressTraining.com

I strongly recommend that you continue with this Action Step by creating a 15-second and one-minute Conscious Calling before moving on to the next Success Strategy so that you will be prepared for any situation. You may want to customize a few depending on the audience.

Most people are not comfortable talking about themselves this way. **_Well, get over it!!_** If you are going to be successful, you MUST be able to promote yourself and your business.

Confidence and certainty are magnets!!

SUCCESS STRATEGY
6
What's So Good About That?

"You can have brilliant ideas, but if you can't get them across, your ideas won't get you anywhere"
Lee Iacocca – former President of Ford Motor Company

We frequently talk to prospects and potential investors about the many features our business has to offer, rather than the benefits. A *feature* is a descriptive phrase about your product or service. For example, "Our event-planning service includes cleanup" or "Our products are hand-made" are features. Feature statements always contain "our" or "we." They are about the product or service, and ultimately, about *you*. Problem is, your customers aren't generally interested in *you* - they are interested in what you can do for *them*. If we are to win people over and help them want to do business with us, it is essential that we focus on what's in it for them - the benefits. A benefit explains what the feature gives them... "One-stop shopping," "The best quality furniture in town" or "Boards that help you play a better game" are all examples of benefit phrases. Benefits explain how your product or service helps your customer. If you are not speaking in terms of benefits, you are missing an important part of communication. When communicating with people, we always want to be talking about what's in it for them.

In this chapter, I'll share a great exercise that I find useful any time I start a new project or marketing campaign. This exercise helps me see how my business will benefit my customers from their perspective.

Use this exercise before creating e-mails, business cards, and websites. If you are not speaking in the form of benefits, then you are missing communication. This simple exercise is something I learned from Bob Circosta of the Home Shopping Network, and it is perfect for developing benefit-driven communication.

ACTION STEP 5: *"WHAT'S SO GOOD ABOUT THAT?"*

"Speak in such a way that others love to listen to you."
— Unknown

1. Make a list of all the things you or your business offers. For example, if you are a business coach, you might offer:

Features		Benefits
One-hour session over the phone	*What's so good about that?*	Easy access from anywhere

MP3 recording of session	*What's so good about that?*	Listen over and over again, don't miss anything. Repetition is key!

Step-by-step action plan	*What's so good about that?*	Easy to follow "To Do" list with dates attached

Expertise from start-up to acquisition	*What's so good about that?*	Concrete guidelines for every business owner, no matter what phase of business growth they are in

Million-Dollar Rolodex	*What's so good about that?*	Contacts for all of your business needs

2. Go back to each item on the list, and ask yourself "What's so good about that?" Think in terms of your customer's needs, and write down every benefit you can think of that ties in to the features you have to offer.

3. Rephrase the brainstormed benefits you have come up with to create "benefit phrases" that you can easily use in e-mail campaigns, website design, business card design, and all other company communication.

Create your own list of feature and benefit phrases here:

Features		Benefits
_____ _____ _____	*What's so good about that?*	_____ _____ _____
_____ _____ _____	*What's so good about that?*	_____ _____ _____
_____ _____ _____	*What's so good about that?*	_____ _____ _____
_____ _____ _____	*What's so good about that?*	_____ _____ _____

Features		Benefits
_____ _____ _____	*What's so good about that?*	_____ _____ _____
_____ _____ _____	*What's so good about that?*	_____ _____ _____
_____ _____ _____	*What's so good about that?*	_____ _____ _____
_____ _____ _____	*What's so good about that?*	_____ _____ _____
_____ _____ _____	*What's so good about that?*	_____ _____ _____

That's Easy!

*"As marketers, we should be changing the mantra from always be closing to **always be helping"***
- Jonathan Lister, LinkedIn.com

SUCCESS STRATEGY
7
Power in Your Bio

"The leader must know, must know that he knows, and must be able to make it abundantly clear to those about him that he knows"   - Clarence B. Randall

In Success Strategy 9, we will discuss the importance of creating Press Kits, and will introduce the 'recipe' for building a successful press kit. Let's spend some time now on preparing your Power Bio - a very important ingredient for your Press Kit. A biography is a detailed description of someone's life. A Power Bio is a compelling one-page document that highlights how you stand out from the competition. Your bio should showcase you without being boring or stuffy.

I have found that many people are challenged when it comes to speaking about themselves. They worry that it will come across as egotism or boasting, but a successful Power Bio helps people get to know you. It will allow you to connect with potential customers and build client trust in your expertise.

When writing your Power Bio, avoid writing about your degrees and educational history. Include any professional designations, awards, and associations. If you have authored any articles or books, include them as well - they serve as subtle third-party endorsements.

Think about how your past has impacted your present. Many times, we do not see how the two are related, but I have found that 9 times out of 10, there is a way to tie our past into our present situation in a powerful way.

Be sure to include some personal information in the last paragraph of your power bio. For example, "Shannon is the proud mom of two wonderful kids. She enjoys supporting them as a 'Band Mom' as they develop their musical talents." This personal touch gives readers some insight into your personality, and makes you appear more approachable and trustworthy.

When I am working with my clients, I take them through a 12-step process. I believe that five of these are essential to creating a powerful personal and professional bio. We will use these five key topics/questions as we build your bio.

Many people do not realize the power of word, but the right word can make a huge difference when a potential client is getting to know you via your Power Bio. We will be using "Power Words" in your bio for maximum impact.

Consider adding a professional photo to your Power Bio for another personal touch. Make sure it is color, and not too small. A good picture is a great way to help prospects get to know you.

If your message is important to you and you want to get it out to the world, then you must spend the time you need to master the Power Bio!

> *"When you brand yourself properly, the competition becomes irrelevant."*
> -Unknown

Let's get to work...

ACTION STEP 6: *FIVE ESSENTIAL KEYS TO A POWER-PACKED PERSONAL & BUSINESS BIO*

Post a separate sheet of paper for each of the following topics/questions on the wall for one week. Write your thoughts and answers on each sheet, adding to them as you go through the week.

1) Think about your field of expertise/scope of recognition or program. What is it about you that makes you wildly successful?

2) List your accolades, awards, titles, grants, special honors, training, and certificates, etc.

3) Why are you different? Consider events of significant importance you have been involved in, something you are #1 or FIRST in, and/or something that gives you historical importance.

4) What obstacle(s) have you overcome? How did you overcome them, and how does that relate to your business?

5) List the REASONS why people need your business and must take action to buy your product or services.

ACTION STEP 7: *POWER WORDS*

Refer to the Power Word list on the next few pages. Select five power words to include in your power bio.

1._____

2._____

3._____

4._____

5._____

POWER WORDS

A accelerated accomplished achieved addressed administered advised allocated answered appeared applied appointed appraised approved arranged assessed assigned assisted assumed assured audited awarded

B bought briefed broadened brought budgeted built

C catalogued caused changed chaired clarified classified closed collected combined commented communicated compared compiled completed computed conceived concluded conducted conceptualized considered consolidated constructed consulted continued contracted controlled converted coordinated corrected counseled counted created critiqued cut

D dealt decided defined delegated delivered demonstrated described designed determined developed devised diagnosed directed discussed distributed documented doubled drafted

E earned edited effected eliminated endorsed enlarged enlisted ensured entered established estimated evaluated examined executed expanded expedited experienced experimented explained explored expressed extended

F filed filled financed focused forecast formulated found founded

G gathered generated graded granted guided

H halved handled helped

I identified implemented improved incorporated increased indexed initiated influenced innovated inspected installed instituted instructed insured interpreted interviewed introduced invented invested investigated involved issued

J joined

K kept

L launched learned leased lectured led licensed listed logged

M made maintained managed matched measured mediated met modified monitored motivated moved

N named navigated negotiated

O observed opened operated ordered organized oversaw

P participated perceived performed persuaded planned prepared presented processed procured programmed prohibited projected promoted proposed provided published purchased pursued

Q qualified questioned

R raised ranked rated realized received recommended reconciled recorded recruited redesigned reduced regulated rehabilitated related reorganized repaired replaced replied reported represented researched resolved responded restored revamped reviewed revise

S saved scheduled selected served serviced set set-up shaped shared showed simplified sold solved sorted sought sparked specified spoke staffed started streamlined strengthened stressed stretched structured studied submitted substituted succeeded suggested summarized superseded supervised surveyed systematized

T tackled targeted taught terminated tested took toured traced tracked traded trained transferred transcribed transformed translated transported traveled treated trimmed tripled turned tutored

U umpired uncovered understood understudied unified unraveled updated upgraded used utilized

V verbalized verified visited

W waged weighed widened won worked wrote

More power suggestions

ability capable capability capacity competence competent complete completely consistent contributions demonstrated developing educated efficient effective effectiveness enlarging equipped excellent exceptional expanding experienced global increasing knowledgeable major mature maturity nationwide outstanding performance positive potential productive proficient profitable proven qualified record repeatedly resourceful responsible results significant significantly sound specialist substantial substantially successful stable thorough thoroughly versatile vigorous well educated well rounded worldwide

ACTION STEP 8: *WRITE <u>YOUR</u> POWER BIO*

Pull together the information you gathered in Action Step 6 and the Power Words you selected in Action Step 7 to write your Power Bio. Have two or three people carefully proofread and edit your bio prior to finalizing it. Be sure to catch and correct any typographical, spelling, and grammatical mistakes, as some prospects may be turned off by them.

Be prepared to revise your Power Bio at *least* every six months to keep it current and interesting. Following is a sample Power Bio to help you as you write your own. When going on the radio or presenting at events, you can utilize a portion of your bio to create a 1-2 minute introduction.

Sample Power Bio

Shannon Burnett-Gronich has come a long way since her days as a single mother of two, struggling to make ends meet. Through her dedicated focus and a deep desire to help others find success, Shannon has emerged as a highly-regarded, multi-faceted business executive. Her legendary training and coaching services plus her event planning, marketing, public relations, and networking skills have been harnessed by celebrities and every-day Joes alike to build their businesses. Her prowess has made her the go-to expert for luminaries like T Harv Eker (Secrets of the Millionaire Mind), Stewart Levine (Resolution Works), and Dr. Gary Null (America's #1 Health Guru).

Shannon has spent more than a decade building an international conscious business community by helping small businesses grow into their full potential through knowledge-sharing, marketing, and cooperative strategies. She has also successfully raised over $1M according to SEC compliance requirements.

Known as the owner of an exclusive "Million Dollar Rolodex," Shannon has successfully attained over $3 Million in F-R-E-E press for herself and her clients. What's more, she readily shows others how to do the same. A master at creating strategic alliances and developing sustainable partnerships, Shannon almost effortlessly resolves multiple, complex issues while motivating teams to peak performance. Shannon has appeared on television, radio, and in the press. She's co-author of the Amazon #1 best seller "Law of Business Attraction - The Secret of Cooperative Success" with T Harv Eker of The Millionaire Mind.

Shannon has produced over 300 events and conferences since 2001 with 100+ exhibitors and 100+ volunteers. And she still has all her hair! In the process she discovered that most event sponsors, speakers, and exhibitors are missing key knowledge and planning skills necessary to make their event successful. This insight led to Shannon's creation of a simple system to train businesses and their teams in the fine art of conference excellence. She guides her clients through customized systems and follow-up implementation that turns leads into cash through investors, joint venture partners, product sales, and sponsors. Her clients get results and make money! Last year she provided multiple group trainings for cities producing the "ReBirth 2012" Barbara Marx Hubbard events globally.

Shannon lives in Florida with her husband, Ari, an elite athletic trainer and rehabilitation specialist; her son, Alex; and her daughter, Makayla, who are both developing musicians and budding conscious entrepreneurs. Recent addition baby Ryan, is adding even more happiness to all of their lives. Some of Shannon's most joyful moments are spent helping Alex and Makayla with their bands as they grow personally and professionally, and watching little Ryan develop and thrive!

That's Easy!

SUCCESS STRATEGY

8
Stand Out from the Competition

"Stop trying to fit in when you were born to stand out"
Movie, "What a Girl Wants" - 2003

Before you can stand out from the competition, you have to be seen. One of the best ways to get you and your business in front of the public is a press release. A press release is a pseudo-news story, always written in third person. Its job is to show an editor or reporter that you, your business, service, or product is newsworthy. Press releases can be in print or on the internet. They can be sent alone, as part of a full press kit, or accompanied by a sales pitch letter.

In this Success Strategy, I will help you write a press release, get it to the right people, and keep it out of the trash.

Press Release Basics

Your press release should be no more than one-page long, double-spaced. The font should be 12-14 in size - easy to read, but not too big. The idea is to get your message across quickly and clearly. If you can't get your message across short, sweet, and simple, then work with your language until you make it work.

Do not put your press release on your letterhead unless your business is Coca-Cola or a national brand. The media is not looking to give away free ads, they are looking for stories that will be interesting to their readers and pleasing to management. Stories that are inspirational, educational, or of human interest are usually good media magnets.

There are several possible formats for creating your press release. We are going to use a simple format with five sections:

☆ Tagline
☆ Introduction
☆ Body
☆ Closing/Call to Action
☆ Contact Details

I suggest that you create a few different press release versions so that you can test them to determine which are the most effective. Send out 5-10 to a variety of media contacts (see Success Strategy 10) to see how well they are received and which work better - attention-grabbing taglines, etc.

Once you have a press release that works, it's all about getting it out and following up on it.

ACTION STEP 9: *TAGLINES THAT SIZZLE*

The tagline is the most important part of a press release. The tagline captures the attention of the readers and allows them to decide whether or not to read the full article. Taglines are useful in many areas of marketing, so work through this process and use it to create subject lines for email, brochures, and websites. You can even use them when speaking with someone to capture their attention.

Here are the 10 most frequently used words in taglines in modern advertising, according to Victor Schwab (one of the sharpest copywriters in the business):

You	**Money**
Your	**Now**
How	**People**
New	**Want**
Who	**Why**

Taglines or titles are best at 5-7 words in length - enough to capture attention, but not enough to lose your audience.

One of the best ways to come up with great taglines is to look at magazines, like Cosmopolitan, that have spent billions of dollars in research to come up with taglines that sell magazines.

Visit your local store or magazine website and check out the magazine covers. Fill in the blanks below using taglines from a few different magazines:

How to_____

Secrets to_____

7 Steps to_____

Strategies to_____

10 Ways to_____

I have found that numbers are the most effective, so if you can use them, do it! Here are sample taglines I have used over the years that have worked very well.

11 Mistakes Even the Smartest Exhibitors Make

85 Ways to Improve Your Health in 6 Hours or Less

How to get $1000's in Free Press

Paralyzed Woman Uses Chinese Exercise to Heal

How to Make Money While You Are Sleeping

Now create 5-6 taglines for your business that you can use in your press release or other marketing endeavors:

1. _____

2. _____

3. _____

4. _____

5. _____

6. _____

We are in a world where people are really focused on news and negative things that are happening in the world. I strongly suggest that we focus on using positive and uplifting language in taglines. Don't use complex or complicated language, as it can be confusing.

Let me share a story that demonstrates the importance of effective taglines. A few years ago, Stewart Levine of ResolutionWorks.org hired me to promote and produce a few events for him. This man is absolutely amazing, and his work is a 9-step agreement process that yields wonderful results.

It is so profound for any business or individual to use in all areas of their life to create sustainable relationships and partnerships. Originally, Mr. Levine wanted to use the title "Creating Sustainable Partnerships" as his marketing tagline. Getting people to enroll in his first class was like pulling teeth! Prior to his next event, I changed the tagline to "Avoid the Pitfalls of Unclear Agreements," and the class filled effortlessly! Exact same curriculum, just a different tagline.

ACTION STEP 10: *THE "PROBLEM"*

The next step in writing a powerful press release is the introduction. This is almost as important as the tagline, as it must follow up on the 'grab' of the tagline and continue to capture the reader's attention. The introduction is usually 2-3 sentences long and focuses on 'the problem.' The most effective introductions use credible stats to support your premise. If, for some reason, you cannot find the right statistics, a quote from a well-known, credible expert can also be used.

Select two of the taglines you wrote in the previous step, and write introductions that support them and continue to hold the reader's attention. It is best to focus on using numbers, statistics, and facts to emphasize 'the problem.'

ACTION STEP 11: *THE "SOLUTION"*

The next section of the press release is the body. In this section, we start to introduce "the solution." Always quote yourself as an expert in the body. The body should be 5-7 sentences long, depending on the rest of the press release. Keep in mind that the press release needs to fit on a single page, double spaced.

Quoting yourself might look something like *"Every successful person has a coach" states Shannon Gronich, Amazon #1 Best Selling Author and business coach "to help them navigate from an outside perspective."* You can see that I put my name in the middle with my statement in quotes.

The body of the press release should provide a few specific solutions. For example, if your tagline is "101 Ways to Market Your Business for Free," you should provide one or two of the "101 Ways" in the body. Offer the others as a free report on your website... or something similar.

Write one or two body paragraphs for your press release. Focus on providing solutions and quoting yourself as an expert in your field.

ACTION STEP 12: *CALL TO ACTION*

The closing and 'Call to Action' is another vital part of your press release. The closing summarizes, wraps up, and invites the reader to DO something. The closing paragraph is typically 2-3 sentences long, and includes an invitation to join something, make a difference by supporting something, or receive something - but the reader MUST take action to see results.

Here is a sample of a 'Call to Action':

"By providing your audience with information about this 10th Annual Community Event, we can work together to change lives and contribute to a healthier community. Join us February 21, 2010 for the expo being held at the Broward County Convention Center, for a one-day rejuvenation."

Create your own Closing/Call to Action, inviting your reader to join, make a difference, or receive something - but make them take action and work for it!

ACTION STEP 13: *CONTACT DETAILS*

The final piece in the 'press release puzzle' is contact details. You want to be sure that the media and all prospects know who they need to contact to find out more.

Finish your press release by including the following contact details:

Name:
Email:
Phone:
Website:

If you press release is about an event remember to include the date, time, and the location with the contact details.

To help you as you write your press release, here are the 16 Most Persuasive Words you can use in a press release, according to David Ogilvy, the "Father of Advertising":

1. Suddenly
2. Now
3. Announcing
4. Introduction
5. Improvement
6. Amazing
7. Sensational
8. Remarkable
9. Revolutionary
10. Startling
11. Miracle
12. Magic
13. Offer
14. Quick
15. Challenge
16. Wanted

Sample press release:

85 Ways to Improve Your Health in 8 Hrs or Less

According to best-selling author Paul Pilzner, "The wellness industry is on the verge of changing our lives as much as the automobile and the personal computer industries did." With the exciting changes in how we view our health taking hold, everyone should be aware of choices for their health.

"The average person is confused by our healthcare system and treating symptoms," says Shannon Burnett founder and CEO of Conscious Living Space and producer of Expo of Heart. "By spending just one day at the Expo of Heart in Ft Lauderdale, the community can find over 85 opportunities to connect with leading practitioners, products, and services that can change lives."

By providing your audience with information about this 10th Annual Community Event, together we can change lives and contribute to a healthier community.

Contact: Shannon Burnett-Gronich at 321-549-2128

When: Sunday, February 21, 10 AM-6 PM

Where: Broward County Convention Center

What: Expo of Heart – FREE spinal checks, FREE massage & food samples, Special Expo only LOW COST Health Screenings, 100+ Exhibitors, 50+ hours of workshops

Sample press release:

Time Magazine's "New Mr. Natural" Comes to Melbourne

Gary Null holds a Ph.D. in human nutrition and public health science. He is a multi award-winning journalist and New York Time bestselling author. Dr. Null currently has the longest airing syndicated radio show "Natural Living with Gary Null", which has earned 21 Silver Microphone Awards.

"Alternative medicine and healing is becoming a more standard practice these days," says Shannon Burnett-Gronich, event producer and natural health advocate, "through his education to thousands of people on how to lead healthier lives." The award-winning film producer and author is in town to premiere his new movie, "Love" in which Dr. Null and other experts in psychology and spirituality, and philosophers focus on relationships and the most powerful force in the universe – Love.

Join us for this movie premier followed by Q & A with Dr. Null himself. As a gift for attendees, Dr. Null is gifting a FREE Book, "Living in the Moment – Prescription for the Soul" and a DVD, "Preventing and Reversing Diabetes Naturally" ($64 value). To register, call 321-549-2128 or go to GaryNull.com for more information.

Contact: Shannon Burnett-Gronich

Info: info@ShannonBurnett.com or 321-549-2128

When: Sunday, June 13, 2010 – 2:00 -6:00 PM

Where: Crowne Plaza Oceanfront in Indialantic, Florida

Media Magic

SUCCESS STRATEGY
9
Don't Miss the Boat

"Whatever you focus on happens, so put energy into marketing daily and consider it done." - Shannon Burnett-Gronich

You have now successfully identified several ways that you can utilize marketing opportunities for your growing business. You understand the importance of sharing your message in terms of benefits, not features. You are ready to share that message through your Conscious Calling, or Elevator Speech, and you have written your Power Bio and at least one Press Release.

Now we will look at another important way you can become a magnet for free marketing - a press kit. With a press kit available, you will be ready for any *Media Magic* opportunities that come your way. A press kit for success should always include your Power Bio, Press Releases, Press Clippings, Photos, Marketing Collateral (brochures, etc), Order Forms, and a Price List.

You will want to have several different press kits available. Each kit may vary, depending on whom you will be sharing it with and what kind of media requests you get. In this boot camp, we will focus on two key parts of the press kit: the power bio and press releases.

You want to be sure that your press kit is available in soft copy, for use online, and in hard copy format, ready to mail out on a moment's notice. Purchase quality, professional folders with business card slots to organize each press kit.

ACTION STEP 14: CREATE YOUR PRESS KIT

Begin by gathering any prior marketing collateral you have used or prepared, as well as any media exposure, including:

- Articles you have written
- Articles written about you
- Presentations and speaking engagements
- Other related press clippings
- Power Bio
- Press Release(s)
- Business Cards
- Price Lists & Order Forms
- Company marketing pieces - ESSENTIAL!

Make sure your company brochures, business cards, and other marketing materials have a similar look and feel. This will help brand you, making you easily recognizable to customers and prospects. It will also give your press kits (and you!) a more professional look.

Have Action Photos Ready!

I missed a huge opportunity for *Media Magic* when a reporter asked for a photo and all I had was a headshot. Now headshots are very important and they should be updated yearly, but *action photos* are really what they want. Keep in mind, these do not have to be 'big' action photos. One *Media Magic* opportunity I did seize used an action photo of me, looking down and pointing at a brochure (see below). Simple, with just a little movement and interest, but it got me a half a page of free press! Be certain that your photos are high resolution, because newspapers and magazines cannot print lower quality photos. Don't even try to pull a picture off a website for print use - it will end up grainy and pixelated.

Showcase Yourself!

How are you currently showcasing yourself? Do you have a website and/or blog? Are you a featured contributor to another company's website or print media? If not, seek out opportunities to get out there! Be sure to include copies of all of your work in your press kit.

If you don't have any prior marketing exposure, you have a tremendous opportunity for growth! Start now, using the skills and techniques you have learned from this book. Start a blog, submit articles to local publications, and seek out speaking engagements and presentation opportunities.

Always get copies of any media exposure, including ads you pay for. If you have been interviewed on the radio, your media kit should have a copy of the interview on a CD.

Media Magic

SUCCESS STRATEGY

10

It's a Numbers Game

*"It's a numbers game – the more you send out,
the more response you get"* - Susan Scott

Now that you have read through each of the Success Strategies and completed each of the Action Steps in this book, you are ready for the next step - getting your message to those who will help you get it out to the public. Remember that it's a numbers game - the more contacts you make, the more *Media Magic* opportunities you will have!

The key to success in this Success Strategy is to have a focused plan, as you have with every other process you have learned.

ACTION STEP 15: *GET YOUR MESSAGE OUT!*

Develop a media contact list. There are ways of buying lists, but it is much more cost-effective to develop your own list.

1. Determine which area of the media you want to focus on. For example, if your business is sales and production of Bag Toss games, your media focus might be sports, recreation, and games. Do your 'due diligence' and locate media contacts in print (newspapers, magazines, etc), television, radio, and the internet.

2. Start a spreadsheet in Excel or your preferred software, with headings for:

- Media company name
- Individual contact name
- Contact phone number
- Contact street address
- Contact email address
- Deadline dates

Be sure to indicate their preferred contact method as well. You may need to use the other methods initially, but will want to focus on their preference as you move forward.

Reporters and producers make great media contacts. Freelance writers are another great avenue, as they have contacts in many areas. Pick up the newspaper and pay attention to radio and television. Don't forget to ask your friends "Who do you know in the media?" All of these are opportunities for *Media Magic!*

3. Begin making contact with a phone call first. Let them know that you have a story they may be interested in. Share a tagline or tell them just enough to peak their interest. Ask them to whom you should speak regarding press release submission. The key here is to build a relationship quickly while being conscious of their time. I typically ask, "Am I calling at a good time?"

After I get their permission to send the press release, I ask for permission to follow up to be certain they received it. When I follow up, I *always* expect them to say they don't have it, or haven't gotten to it. Patience is key here! Expect this to happen several times. Remember that your contacts are very busy, and the more kindness and understanding you demonstrate, the more successful you will be. I often say, "You must be super busy. How long have you worked here?" I get them talking about themselves as quickly as possible.

Take notes on your spreadsheet as you follow up, indicating concerns and progress.

How to Win Friends and Influence People *by Dale Carnegie* © has sold millions of copies and is my favorite book. It shares great ways to sincerely connect with others and is a wonderful reference when trying to reach out to the media or prospects.

That's Easy!

Media Magic

BONUS CHAPTERS

Media Magic

SUPPLEMENTAL BONUS CHAPTERS
Life-Long Learning

"All of the top achievers I know are life-long learners... looking for new skills, insights, and ideas... "
- Denis Waitley

When leading authorities in press releases, public speaking, and social media offered to contribute their expertise to *Media Magic*, I was thrilled! These supplemental chapters provide even more great information to help you and your business excel in today's highly competitive environment.

Paula Langguth Ryan's *Tips for Writing Big-Value Supersonic Press Releases from a Press Release Junkie* provides a look at writing a press release from the viewpoint of editors and other media professionals. Her pointed questions will help you fine-tune your press releases into stories media professionals will jump at.

If You're Not Effectively Communicating Your Ideas, It's Literally Costing You Your Dreams! by AmondaRose Igoe contributes three Speaking Breakthrough Strategies that will help you reach your true speaking potential and improve your ability to communicate – in front of a large group or in a one-on-one interview.

Social Media Made Simple is Jerry Hayward's guide to effectively using social networks like Facebook and Twitter. These "must use" networks can complement your existing marketing plan by taking advantage of the growing number of customers who spend hours a day sharing their information and making connections online.

Inside-Out Marketing for Brand Acceleration introduces a multi-pronged approach to brand acceleration. With six insight-driven strategies, Donna Anselmo helps you consider your own brand through a set of lenses that enhance insight and speed you to better results. In this chapter, you will explore what drives your brand, consider issues underlying your brand's performance, and learn how to build your brand and accelerate its growth.

The World's Greatest Business Card by Keith Leon shares how to position yourself as an expert and grow your business by authoring a book. Learn the five advantages of being a published author and the benefits of using your book as your business card. Keith's goal is to help you create the book you always wanted to write and finish it fast!

Take full advantage of the advice, tips, and techniques these domain experts provide. Read their chapters thoroughly, work through any exercises they suggest, and put the results to work for you. Remember to always keep learning to grow closer and closer to excellence!

SUPPLEMENTAL BONUS CHAPTER
1
Tips for Writing Big-Value Supersonic Press Releases, from a Press Release Junkie
by Paula Langguth Ryan

Just before the turn of the millennium, I took a job as executive editor for a Baltimore newspaper. It started out as a favor. The publisher was a longtime friend and his editor had moved overseas to write a book. Before long, our content was the talk of the country. We were even named America's most-award winning non-daily paper. It takes major work to fill a bi-weekly newspaper with writing that makes people want to read beyond the headlines. I had a small staff as well, so it wasn't like we were roaming the streets day and night tracking down stories on our own. The secret to my success never took me farther than my desk.

The truth is: ***I was a press release junkie***. I became adept at spotting worthy news stories and feature ideas that were buried in well-written (and not so well-written) press releases. Between the US Postal Service, our thermal fax (yes, I'm dating myself here), and e-mail, we probably received 100-200 press releases daily from people wanting to get news coverage for their product, service, or event.

When you're on deadline, every millisecond counts! So you scan headlines first, then opening paragraphs. You quickly learn to spot your go-to people. You recognize who is shoving worthy stories under your nose and who's shoveling something else. I knew the quicker I could find the gems in the pile of mail, the quicker I could get the printing presses running. In addition, the more stories I could pull from press releases, the less I had to pay stringer writers, which always made my expense-conscious publisher happy!

When I reviewed press releases, I made a mental list of who wrote strong copy and who wrote dry copy. I could spot press releases that were clearly buckshot attempts being sent to every possible publication, versus those that were sniper sharp – geared directly toward our readers. I could smell those who were desperate to get mentioned in our paper and those who were eager to give our readers something of value. This last group was the folks I looked for first in each day's press release flurry.

You know what editors like best? Being able to pick up a press release, edit it for style and content as if it had come in from a familiar writer, and pop it into an empty space in the paper. The same goes for radio and TV producers. You know how I know this? Because long before I was an editor, I was a copywriter - and I specialized in getting my clients free press from my press releases. My press releases got placed as "stories" in everything from local newspapers to Cosmopolitan magazine. Editors usually picked up what I'd written and ran with it without changing a word. Radio personalities were giddy to announce my events because the copy was entertaining and easy to read. TV producers loved my press releases because I always included samples that could be easily demonstrated for their viewers.

My favorite TV coverage was a segment on eco-friendly products. My client's product was clearly visible on the desk for five full minutes while the show hosts talked about all the unique benefits of my client's product and how it tied into the local environmental issues, and then briefly mentioned all the other products. The entire time, one show host kept playing with my client's product even when they talked about the other products. The message was clear: "this product is engaging and worthy of your attention." ***Any idea how much five minutes of advertising on the same network news channel would have cost?***

The difference between all of the products was in their press releases. My client's press release gave the newscasters a ***story*** they could run with. The other press releases merely gave out information. The words you use in your news releases, press releases, and PSAs (public service announcements) are what make your product, service, or event an anchor for any media story.

Spoon feed your media outlets. Hand them a story on a silver platter. Show, don't tell. Give, don't try to get. Share benefits, not features. Tie your story to something newsworthy or timely in a way that is fresh and edgy. (You've heard all that before, and if you read on you'll find specific examples of *exactly* how to do this yourself.)

Create such a strong case without even mentioning what you're pitching that the only conclusion the media professional can make is that **you** are the solution to what ails them! And what ails them is their desire to fill their time and pages with attention-grabbing and entertaining stories that speak to their audience.

When I was doing Break the Debt Cycle workshops nationwide, my press release *Three Tips to Stop Being a Slave to MasterCard* often got picked up verbatim in local newspapers. **Way better to have a half-page article that sets the stage for your event and makes people want to come learn more from you in person, than a mere three lines in a calendar listing, yes?**

When Jaime Wooten, creator of *The Golden Girls* television show, premiered a new play in his hometown of Goldsboro, NC, our press release got my client so much coverage on local radio, TV, and newspapers, the entire show run was sold out.

Below are three examples of what I'm talking about when it comes to the power of the copy you write. These should get your creative juices flowing!

1. When we built a spiritual center in a former funeral home, this is the opening of the press release that nabbed us a feature story with photographs:

> **What happens when you combine an abandoned funeral parlor with an inspired group of people?**
> **A lot of spirits get raised – and we're not talking ghosts.**

Last summer and fall, when twenty people gathered in Cocoa Village to turn the abandoned Wylie-Baxley funeral parlor into a Sunday night spiritual playhouse, more than a few eyebrows were raised. In the end, months of elbow grease and high spirits transformed the abandoned building into a showcase for The Village Gathering.

"We wanted to experience joy together, to get away from the dogma and focus on how we're alike rather than how we differ," said co-inspirator Rosalie Bianco.

Don't expect any staid church service here. This group is irreverent and willing to poke fun at themselves as they encourage us all to take personal responsibility for the lives we've created.

After a successful trial run last year, The Village Gathering is back stronger than ever with a season of Sunday night programs that includes interfaith conversations with Christian, Muslim, and Hindu leaders; inspirational concerts by national artists; thought-provoking and inspiring films and documentaries and special interfaith events including a Metaphysical Passover. The first Sunday of every month is the high-energy *Sunday Night Alive!* production.

Not only did we get a feature story about the Passover Seder – we also nabbed a follow up story with pictures about a county-wide Cosmic Mass event we sponsored!

2. In 2004, the International Association of Professional Organizers was looking for recognition as the leader in setting industry standards. This press release (which was immediately issued after a national talk show featured an organizer from the "other" main association) got picked up all across the country, including in Cosmo magazine. Here's how it opened:

What's in YOUR Organizer's Closet?

Organizing, like any other industry, has good and bad professionals. For example, one professional organizer, as seen on Dr. Phil, was so disorganized you could barely walk through her house. Dirty diapers clung to her couch and amidst her clutter she often couldn't find bills that needed paying, or her own phone. If you knew you were hiring a professional organizer whose home looked like that, would you really want them to organize you?

Avoiding that kind of situation is why it's important to know what level of experience, competency, education, and trustworthiness your organizer possesses. That's why we recommend you use the International Association of Professional Organizers' Global Referral Network, which is customized like no other organizing industry referral network.

It must have been a strong headline – the PR department handling Capital One credit cards soon after launched a huge campaign whose "What's in *your* wallet?" tag line may sound familiar.

3. Every year around the holidays, we trot out the same winning press release and get amazing coverage repeatedly:

Free guide gets you home for the holidays even if you have no credit

On a recent business trip, Paula Langguth Ryan arrived at the rental car agency about 10 PM. The couple in front of her was clearly frustrated. They had no credit card and wanted to pay cash. They were willing to pay the extra deposit needed, but they didn't know they would have to show a copy of their insurance card or pay for the rental company's insurance. The situation eventually escalated and the manager escorted the couple from the building without a car.

They could have avoided the frustration and been happily on their way to enjoying their trip if they'd known about *How to Travel Without Credit*. This 8-page free special report from consumer bankruptcy expert Paula Langguth Ryan is designed for people with no credit.

"With a record number of people going bankrupt again this year, millions no longer have credit available. Many are joining the growing cash-only revolution. This doesn't always make travel easy, especially holiday travel," says Ryan author of *BOUNCE BACK FROM BANKRUPTCY: A STEP-BY-STEP GUIDE TO GETTING BACK ON YOUR FINANCIAL FEET* (4th ed., CM Press, 800/507-9244, PaulaLangguthRyan.com).

The report contains specific strategies for traveling without credit for all major hotels, rental car agencies, and airlines. While airlines have become more flexible about accepting debit cards, hotels and rental car companies aren't as helpful.

To ease the stress of traveling without credit, and to help you get home for the holidays, Ryan offers these helpful tips.

A good press release is timeless, like a black pea jacket or a set of pearls.

Go back and reread the snippets from the above press releases again. Pay attention to the copy. Then grab a press release you're working on for your company. What do your words tell the reader? Make sure it's not about YOU. Make sure it's all about THEM. And what they can expect. It should be tight. ***Positive. Uplifting. Easy-reading. No spare words. No excess self-praise. Draw a picture.***

With your press release in hand, grab a pen and three different colored highlighters. Then ask yourself these questions about your writing:

1. Does your headline draw a powerful picture for your reader? If not, write down 10 possible headlines you can think of that DO draw a picture.

1. _____
2. _____
3. _____
4. _____
5. _____
6. _____
7. _____
8. _____

2. Which information in your press release gives your readers something valuable? Mark these up in one color. What can you do to enhance the value even more?

_____
_____
_____
_____

3. Where's your weak copy? What words, phrases, or sentences stop the flow of your reading? If you're too close to the copy, have someone read the copy aloud. If they stumble, mark those places in another color. (Preferably red so you immediately know these folks have got to go!)

_____
_____
_____
_____

4. Where have you demonstrated a need and then showed how what *you* offer can fill that need? Highlight those in another color. Where can you strengthen these to draw an even stronger picture?

_____
_____
_____
_____

5. What do the quotes in your press releases do to make the picture even stronger or tell the story in greater detail?

_____

_____

_____

_____

6. What **haven't** you told your readers that would complete the picture? Write that information down off the top of your head. Don't try and "craft" your writing. Write as if you're talking to your best friend, or your mom. Imagine they've asked you a question and want a plain English example as an answer.

_____

_____

_____

_____

Learn to write copy that gives your audience value - rather than copy designed to get you results. By extending value with every word you write, you'll get the coverage (and the results) you're looking for. And it will be more far reaching than if you send out press releases that basically jump up and down begging editors and producers to "Look at me! Look at me!"

And remember: Press releases aren't the only way to get free press with powerful copy. Letters to the editors and blog posts and comments on other people's blogs can also get you free publicity. So can a Tweet. Or a Facebook post. So can your website copy, your brochure copy, heck, even your menus if you own a restaurant!

The quickest way to build strong copy is to take an old press release and tame the wild and wooly copy that didn't get strong results. If you don't think you're a strong writer, find someone who is. And study the press releases other people put out. Pay attention to which ones are B-O-R-I-N-G and which ones excite the hell out of you and make you want to take an action. Then paper your walls with these examples so you only have to glance up to be reminded how to craft strong copy for your press releases.

 **Paula Langguth Ryan** is a marketing consultant, former financial editor for Phillips Publishing and ghostwriter for national copywriting and finance publishing companies and writers. Ryan has appeared on WOR Radio Network (The Dolans), NPR's WEEKEND EDITION, PBS' "FINANCIAL FREEDOM," NBC's "TODAY IN NEW YORK," and ABC's, "STRESS FREE FINANCE."

Ryan is an internationally-renowned conflict resolution consultant and speaker who believes every communication leaves behind a fingerprint of our own insecurities and concerns. Her powerful communication and CopyTamer® consulting services have been used by clients from a wide range of industries who are gung ho to increase the sales and customer desire for their products and services. Her techniques are proven to work in any imaginable business setting.

She is the creator of the **Vibrational Language of Prosperity Program** which helps you stop communicating in old scarcity language and start speaking in a new empowering language that draws to you the results you want. She is also the creator of the **Supersonic Prosperity-Oriented Copywriting System** which helps demonstrate how to create communications that ooze with self-confidence and self-worth in ways that truly get people to realize this truth: *What you are providing is what they deeply desire!*

Follow Ryan on Facebook **@PaulaLangguthRyan** or Twitter **@CopyTamer**. Visit **PaulaLangguthRyan.com** or call 970-590-3732 or to schedule a free 30 minute consultation or explore having Paula "tame" a piece of existing copy you currently use.

Vibrational Language of Prosperity Program:
PaulaLangguthRyan.com/shop/vibrational-language
Supersonic Prosperity-Oriented Copywriting System:
PaulaLangguthRyan.com/shop/supersonic-copywriting

Supplemental Chapter
2

If You're Not Effectively Communicating Your Ideas, It's Literally Costing You Your Dreams!
by AmondaRose Igoe

Since you started applying what you have learned in the *Media Magic* program, your life is drastically changing in a positive way. You can now picture yourself stepping into the spotlight. You are receiving a never-ending flow of speaking and media opportunities. They are literally pouring in! A local news station wants to interview you tomorrow, you just got booked for an internationally-recognized speaking event, and a national radio station has just set a date with you to showcase you in two weeks. ***Now what?***

Whether you are being interviewed by the media, from print to radio to television, or speaking to an audience of 20 to 2000, you are speaking in public. Many people don't realize that public speaking is not just for presentations, it is something we do every day. Now that you are stepping into the public eye in a much bigger way, this is where speaking success really matters.

First, the BAD news: The reality is that you can know everything about any topic, even your own business or personal transformation. However, if you are unable to communicate effectively, you will ***never*** have the level of true success you ultimately want.

Now, for the GOOD news: By learning from a Public Speaking Expert and Best Selling Author, you can reach your true speaking potential and improve your ability to communicate whether it is in front of a large group, or, simply, a one-on-one interview. Essential to your success is your desire to change and grow.

By identifying and improving your ability to speak in public, you can attain the true success you desire and deserve. Reading this is a great way to start. Whether it is an impromptu interview or a lengthy presentation, ***this will change the way you speak in public forever.***

SPEAKING BREAKTHROUGH STRATEGY # 1

The Three Essential "P's"

"Preparation, integrity, commitment, and dedication to being your best are essential keys to public speaking success."
- AmondaRose Igoe

Have you ever tried to create a presentation or prepare for an interview last minute? Did you stumble and bumble over your words? Did you make the points you wanted to in the right order? Or did you forget half of the good stuff you had wanted to say? Do you live by the philosophy that it is better to "wing it" than be prepared? As a result of "winging it," are you getting the results you desire?

My 3 Essential P's are really quite simple. Are you ready? Here they are: The 3 P's essential to becoming an extraordinary speaker are:

1. **Practice...**
2. **Practice, and then...**
3. **Practice some more!**

I can't believe that so many people forget to do this. Commit to yourself, today, that you are going to Practice, Practice, and then, Practice some more. It is time to say good-bye to "winging it" forever! Practice in your car, practice in front of the mirror, practice while you're working-out, practice everywhere you possibly can. If you take this simple principle and apply it consistently, you ***will*** reap outstanding rewards.

Coaches' Corner

I had to find a unique way. When I started doing presentations over a decade ago, I realized that I had to uncover a way to learn and remember my presentations that worked for me. I knew that trying to memorize my presentation wasn't a smart option. I will discuss memorizing in detail in Part 4.

Here is a simple process that will help you learn your presentation. Remember, you still have to practice, practice, and practice. Realize there are no quick fixes. This does work!

1. Write out your entire presentation or interview questions and answers word for word.

2. Number your pages or index cards (just in case you drop them).

3. Highlight key words to help you focus on key points.

4. Practice it two to three times this way.

5. Decrease the number of words used. You can keep your highlighted words or decrease some of those too.

6. Practice it two to three times this way.

7. Decrease the number of words again. Keep the necessary highlighted words.

8. Practice it two to three times this way. Trust your memory.

9. Decrease and trust until you can present your entire presentation or nail the interview using only a few key words to trigger your memory.

This does take faith and trust. You just need to remember the key words to keep you on track and to help you if you get stuck. It has always worked for me and my clients. It can absolutely work for you. When we give our memory the proper tools, it is more powerful than most of us believe.

SPEAKING BREAKTHROUGH STRATEGY #2

Be Uniquely You!

"Let the audience see the real you. An audience will know when you are faking it." - AmondaRose Igoe

Have you ever tried to model yourself after other speakers? For many reasons, this is a wonderful idea, and a good beginning. However, I found it vital to my own success to incorporate my own unique style. I am uniquely AmondaRose. You are uniquely **YOU**!

While you must learn ***the art*** of public speaking and clear communication, never ever lose your individuality when you speak! By being your authentic self, you will leave a lasting impression in the hearts and minds of your audience.

Remember to honor who you are! Acknowledge what is great about you! There is no one else exactly like you. You have had your own experiences, challenges, setbacks, and success. That is what makes you connect with your audience as the real person you are. Connecting with yourself, knowing your own heart, and sharing the "unique you" with your audience, can create the kind of extraordinary speeches I know you're capable of.

Coaches' Corner

A. We all are unique in our own perfect way. List 5 ways that you are "personally" unique: i.e. funny, dynamic, approachable or a great story teller.

1._____

2._____

3._____

4._____

5._____

B. List 5 ways your presentation topic or message is unique, exceptional, special, or rare: such as the latest technology, fastest delivery time, new perspective, or life transforming.

1._____

2._____

3._____

4._____

5._____

When you are gearing up for your next presentation or interview, I want you to focus on what makes you and your message unique. Be willing to stand out from the competition!

SPEAKING BREAKTHOUGH STRATEGY #3

Become a Question Champion

"Extraordinary speakers know what they have to offer and are willing to stand behind it." - AmondaRose Igoe

You can spot a *"Question Champion"* from far away. Their head is held high. They are standing proud and tall. You notice something is different about them. They are confident and assured because they just won the battle of their life. They survived the question and answer section of their last presentation or interview.

You might be thinking "AmondaRose, it can't be that bad." Believe me it can. There are other factors involved, including how controversial your topic is. No matter what, every speaker must be 100% prepared and ready for whatever questions come their way. If not, an audience or an interviewer is ready and willing to take them down.

If you remain in control and are able to address the questions successfully, you will gain an immense amount of credibility with your audience and interviewer.

Here are few things you must know before you can become a *Question Champion*.

Decide in advance for Live Presentations. Having a question and answer section of your presentation is not a requirement of public speaking. You need to have clear guidelines with your audience stating what is expected for questions. Decide in advance how you plan on handling the Q&A. Choose one of these guidelines and communicate this clearly to your audience.

1. Invite them to see you directly at the end of the meeting or contact you via a website or e-mail address if they have any questions.
2. Dedicate a specific time in your presentation to address audience questions.
3. Allow the guests to ask you questions, during the presentation, as needed.

Coaches' Corner

The Art of Q&A. If you are choosing to answer questions during your actual presentation or you are being interviewed, success will certainly follow if you apply these essential *"Question Champion" strategies.*

1. **Pay attention to the time**. Establish yourself as the authority by staying in control of your presentation and your time. Be conscious of how much time you have for Q & A. If you need to move on, let the audience know that you will address any future questions at end of the meeting.
2. **Listen and repeat.** The success of this portion of your presentation or interview is dependent on your ability to listen. You must listen carefully to the question, restate the question to ensure that you are clear, and check in with the audience to ensure they heard the question. When you have finished answering the question, check in with the person who asked the question to make certain they are satisfied, and then do the same with the audience.
3. **Prepare answers in advance.** You always want to do your best to prepare in advance. Write down 10 of the most common questions that you are asked, and prepare a clear and concise answer for each so that you can deliver with ease each and every time.
4. **Get ready for the curve ball.** On occasion, you may get a confrontational and angry audience member or media

interviewer. They can really challenge a less experienced speaker. Be prepared to address their question with absolute confidence and back it up with a calm demeanor. When you hold your own in those tough situations, you will win them over time and time again. Remember to never let them see you sweat!

AmondaRose Igoe, the 6-Figure Speaking Goddess, has dedicated her life to helping business owners, entrepreneurs, and visionary leaders utilize the power of speaking to create more money, clients, and breakthroughs in their business. As an Award Winning 6-Figure Speaking Expert and Best Selling Author, AmondaRose specializes in helping business owners attract more clients and income with speaking by showing them how to design, deliver, and book speaking engagements. The power of what AmondaRose teaches has helped her clients from around the globe including North America, Germany, Switzerland, England, Romania, and Australia.

AmondaRose is the author of Pain-Free Public Speaking, a contributing author in the number #1 Best Selling book series "Chicken Soup for the Soul," and was a featured expert on the FOX 4 Television Station. AmondaRose has a unique ability to help others connect with the mind, heart, and spirit of their audiences which makes her a highly sought after professional speaker, public speaking trainer, and coach. Whether AmondaRose is being interviewed on television or speaking to international audiences, she ignites the atmosphere with her empowering message, contagious enthusiasm, and real results.

Follow AmondaRose on Facebook at
Facebook.com/AmondaRoseIgoe. Visit **AmondaRose.com** or call **Toll-Free (800) 610-9056** to discover your next 6-figure speaking step.

SPEAKING BLOCKS AND BREAKTHROUGHS
Free public speaking video and audio training that includes:

✓ Simple tools you can use right now that will improve your speaking results **quickly and easily**.

✓ How to find the speaking courage to **stop playing small** and hiding out.

✓ Shift your money mindset so you can increase your income and **help even more people**!

✓ 4 Irresistible speaking strategies to help you **break through your income ceiling.**

Whether you are currently speaking or want to utilize speaking to **grow your business**, you can get the expert help that you need from AmondaRose Igoe, the 6-Figure Speaking Goddess, Award Winning Speaking Expert, and Best Selling Author. Get ready to quickly and easily achieve a new level of speaking success!

Supplemental Chapter
3
Social Media Made Simple
by Jerry Hayward

To the average business owner, social media is perceived as big, "bad," and for the most part, scares people away; at least that's what some people tell me.

Social media is fun, a little addictive, and a useful, powerful tool once you have tamed the Tiger.

Let's talk about this "Tiger" for a moment. A majority of social networks are nothing more than a place to get together, talk and share stuff. You are free to read other user's posts, view their groups, pages, images etc. You can reconnect with old friends, classmates, relatives and just like life offline, refuse to talk to anyone you don't want to.

Another question I hear people ask who are not on social networks is, "Why would you want to waste time doing that?" or "I don't use social media now, why should I bother with it?", I never seem to get to answer them, so I'm going to answer them here.

The reason people *want* to use a social network is its fun, cheap (most are free!), informative -- and did I mention **fun**? Connecting with people from your past, "following" a news story, campaign, or event as it happens, subscribing to news that you want to read, and anything else you find interesting this is what social media is all about. You can control a bunch of different aspects, from what you read, talk about, learn about, and share with others.

There are lots of social networks out there, but for this chapter I am only going to talk about the two biggest ones -- Facebook and Twitter. Almost everything I teach you about these two social networks will apply to other social networks as well.

Twitter: Technically, Twitter is a Micro-Blog which allows you to make a post of up to 140 characters. What this means is that people who want to share what they are doing, enter short messages (tweets), and people who are interested in what they are talking about "follow" them. Twitter's interface consists of users posting text, links and images. If you like what someone tweeted (posted), you can re-tweet it (repost it) and tag them by hash tagging use their username. You can also use hashtags to join discussions and share your insight on hot topics, for example, if you have used a social network you might have seen "#Fun" or "#GameNight". That's what Twitter is all about.

Facebook: Facebook is a slightly more advanced version of Twitter. While Twitter is very simple to understand and use, Facebook has a lot more options -- so in learning to use Facebook, take it slow and be patient. Posts can be longer and they can contain links, games, pictures and videos. On Facebook, there are games, applications, groups, contests, pictures, videos, and lots of ways to customize your experience. Responses to posts are grouped together and in a list format, and you can like, share and comment on what someone else has said or posted. This is similar to re-tweeting on Twitter.

For most people, Facebook is more fun, while Twitter is more informative. Both are informative *and* fun, however.

Getting Started

To get started on Twitter, go to Twitter.com You'll find a sign up form right on the main page. Enter your full name, email address, and a password, and boom, you have a Twitter account.

You don't need to do anything more to start using or posting, but I'd suggest you start following some people. You can find people by clicking "Who to Follow" in the tool bar at the top, once there you can also choose *"Find Friends"* on this page as well -- picking a topic like cars, your church, or a company you like. Enter it into the search, and choose some people to follow from the Twitter accounts that pop up. Then go back to the timeline and see what they have tweeted. If you chose someone interesting, keep them in your follow list. If not, simply click on the word "following", and float over the "Following" button. The button will change and say "Unfollow" and allow you to 'unsubscribe' from their posts from your timeline.

Play with the "Follow" and "Unfollow" functions, and you may find some people you want to keep following. Once you have seen what others have to say, try making some posts of your own -- but only as you feel ready to.

Facebook.com will also let you sign up on the front page. You need to fill in your first and last name, email address, password, date of birth and gender to sign up.

Time

Social media *can* take up a lot of your time. It's *designed* to be addictive, and since the people using the social media site (users) put the content in, the social media site can be as interesting or as dull as the people on it. People who are new to social media will often find that they logged on in the morning to see what was going on, and the whole day just flew by. The average person on social networks spends five hours and thirty-five minutes a day.

Before you get scared, I'm going to tell you how to cut that down. On a side note, let me point out that a lot of retirees, kids, and others with lots of time to kill will spend all day online and drive this average up. Here are some keys to keeping your time online to a reasonable amount:

1. Never use your computer where there isn't a clock.
2. Decide before you log on what you are going to do and for how long.
3. Do it daily (If you let days go by, requests for communication pile up and take more time).
4. Use built-in tools and mobile apps to reduce your time online or automate posts for you.

5. Eliminate groups and people who waste your time online.

I can't stress #5 enough. I had a group request from a friend to join his group, so I was polite and joined. All of a sudden, my email, and phone were buzzing every five minutes, as people sent messages out to all users of this group. However, you can always control what notifications get sent where, reducing interruptions and limiting an excessive amount of email build-up.

Mobile Apps

Mobile apps (programs that run on your smart phone) can be a real timesaver as well as an efficiency enhancer. With a mobile app, you can stay on top of what's going on, when you would otherwise be doing nothing or aren't in front of a computer. Mobile apps also limit which normal desktop options can be used, reducing the temptation to spend a lot of time. I personally do a lot of "Facebooking" with my phone and let my computer automate other things to my account.

Business

If you have a business, I have some specific social media tips for you.

- Being on social media is like being in the phone book; lots of people won't do business with you if they can't find you on a social media network.
- Don't put up anything that you wouldn't put on your cubicle wall. Racy pictures of yourself or significant other, comments about coworkers, employees, and employers have all been a source of pain for their posters.
- Talk about stuff other than, but related to, your company. Pages that are "all business" are boring, and drive away potential friends, employees, and investors. If you are a flag company, for example, talking about history, presidential quotes, and funny laws might keep people coming back to your site (avoid current and recent presidents). Personality is definitely a plus on social media! Keep it fun!

- Automate! The use of "automation tools" can help post things to your social media sites automatically, even when you're busy doing other things, traveling, or vacationing.
- Hire an assistant to keep the site "current".
- Fan pages are great!
- Grow a thicker skin. It's a rough world out there, and you may have some detractors who find your page and post things you wish they hadn't. Remember, ex-customers can be like ex-wives. If you treat them nice they *might* start treating you nice...but not necessarily. Your best defense against detractors will be your on-line friends. Publicly ask for comments from them, and watch unreasonable detractors fade away under the public pressure.

These hints are also good for personal pages because you are sharing with friends *and* that guy who hated you in high school -- all at the same time. Search engines are both your friend **and** your enemy. If you can be found, you can be found by *anyone*. There are ways to limit exposure to your content, both inside and outside of Facebook, but to be on the safe side, always think twice.

Persona

To ensure social networking success, be sure that your accounts are interesting and focused, and that they truly represent you and your business. Bland accounts are not friended, followed, or frequented. Accounts that lack focus and direction often suffer the same fate. Your site needs to reflect you, both as an individual and as a business. Make it interesting! Post pictures of parties -- the kind your mom can attend, pet photos, videos that are in line with your business and personal interests—it's all good! Don't do things that are out of character. Playing FarmVille would be out of character for a technology company, but a business that promotes being back to earth might benefit from having an organic farm attached to it. Think of what other people will see before you post and delete things that are not in character for your persona. Develop your persona, and then be consistent to it for that account.

Tools

Automation in general is a good thing. Find and use tools like AutomaticallyYou, HootSuite, Tweet Later, and Tweet Deck to schedule updates and RSS feeds to and from blogs and news sites you like. These tools can help keep your pages and accounts continually active, boosting your internet rankings. Personally, I use AutomaticallyYou -- but, hey, I'm the founder of the company and think it's a pretty cool tool! Some of these automation tools allow you to schedule the date and time to post messages automatically while you're out doing something else. What a great time saver! Again, tools and automation are a good thing *only* if you can maintain your persona while you use them. Tools that make your account look impersonal or redundant will drive people away.

Manners

I know your mom, like mine, made you practice good manners. It is very important to remember that manners count on the web, too! Using bad manners will cause people to not talk to you, not stay friends with you, or worse yet, start making jokes about you. On the web, your reputation is **everything**.

Let me tell you what *not* to do first:

Posting Without Thinking (PWT): Don't post stuff you don't want everyone to see. Social networks are not the place to gossip. I was in an office where two of the secretaries were gossiping about the boss's wife on a social network. One secretary had to run and get something. Guess who stopped by while the chat window was up on the screen?! Not good.

Don't post negative stuff about work -- period. Jobs have been lost, friendships destroyed, and people really embarrassed because they were guilty of PWT. Don't PWT.

Don't post racy stuff, and keep personal stuff personal. I had a co-worker whose wife posted some racy pictures on his wall.

EVERYONE in the office, including his friends, saw the pictures before he could delete them. Another example of PWT includes a guy who sent me a friend request, then proceeded to post 20 times a day about how *I* needed to go buy something from his site. I dropped him like a hot rock.

Now let's talk about what you should do:

Thinking **_Before_** Posting (TBP), is a good thing. What can you say about others that will make them feel good? Can't think of something? "Liking" or "Re-tweeting" is a simple way to tell someone you are reading their stuff. Posting things to other people's walls is nice, and can help you grow your business. It can also lead to friendship or romance, if that is something you are looking for. *Do* post interesting videos and links to news articles you like. You can be political, but not obnoxiously. Join groups that are interested in topics you are interested in. Write stuff or find articles that you are interested in. If you don't want to, that's fine too. You can just look and read... we call that lurking. People who spend a lot of time on social networks are often lurking 80% of the time, and it's OK to lurk.

When you post, what *should* you post? This is an easy question to answer. Anything that YOU like. Did you see a great cartoon? Scan it in, or link to it online. Did you read a good book? Rate it on Amazon, then link to your rating. Write a poem, tell a joke, give a long lost friend a poke! Make a rhyme, take your time, post a video of a mime! Ok, enough of the Dr. Seuss stuff. The point is, it's not just OK to be quirky, it's a good thing! The more personality you show, the more friends you will have online. Personality is not the same as being obnoxious. Don't pester, defame, or nag people. No one likes that. Most important, just have fun.

So let me recap: Social networks are safe. If you dislike someone, block them and they can't do anything about it. Only talk to people you like or find interesting. Spend as little or as much time as you want on social networks, and take it easy. Most of all, lurk, play, and learn -- all in the comfort of your home or with the convenience of your cell phone. Be careful what you write before posting. Tools are good -- so use them as often as you can. Social networking is all about you and your friends, and whatever makes it easy, fun, and convenient, is a good thing.

See you online!   Jerry

Jerry Hayward is the CEO and founder of AutomaticallyYou, a company that helps people to be consistent in building their online presence by automating their activities on social networks. This patented product is available as a web-based service that runs from your PC. Jerry has written data conversion tools, custom applications for large companies, and shrink-wrapped software for sale. Decided that he wanted to be a programmer at the age of five, Jerry first started programming for pay in high school, then attended the Des Moines Area Community College in their computer science program, spent two years in Taiwan as a missionary, then completed his education at Brigham Young University.

Jerry volunteers regularly as staff at the CEOSpace forum to help entrepreneurs succeed; speaks fluent Mandarin Chinese, and loves science fiction.

Jerry is currently living in American Fork, Utah with his wife Cathy. Jerry is the proud father of five children.

Follow Jerry on Facebook **@automaticallyyou**, and visit **AutomaticallyYou.com** to sign up for your free account. Check out the **AutomaticallyYou Channel** on YouTube for valuable information and tips for your business.

Automatically You

...It's like having more of *you!*

Start marketing like the pros and keep your day job!

Social media is an emerging powerhouse that is making businesses around the world millions every day. Marketing your business through social media can sometimes be a little overwhelming and time-consuming. So many directions and never enough time! Social media is a black hole where time seems to evaporate... Until now!

With AutomaticallyYou.com you can create powerful social media campaigns that run 24/7 *automatically*, and only spend minutes of your time each month.

It's like having a full time social media assistant!

Your marketing messages are sent from your computer, even when you're out doing something else!
Visit **AutomaticallyYou.com** to
sign up for a FREE account!

Supplemental Chapter

4
Inside-Out Marketing for Brand Acceleration
by Donna Anselmo

Introduction

Branding from the inside out is a concept I developed over more than 30 years of strategic branding discussions, brand design, marketing campaigns, internal communications, and public relations work for a broad range of cross-industry clients. I've worked with multi-billion-dollar global leaders, as well as small businesses, not-for-profit organizations, and entrepreneurial ventures. I've worked in industries from banking, education, staffing, and technology to healthcare, wellness, fundraising, and manufacturing. Regardless of the industry or size of client companies, I have identified ten standing principles common to all brand successes.

Ten Branding Principles

1. Programs that enhance employee morale and customer satisfaction play a huge part in brand value. When people on the inside are satisfied and really believe in a product or company, their enthusiasm flows outward. It's like Christmas. The promise of a spectacular experience shines brightly. Customers capture the spirit, and that spirit shines from the inside out. So does a brand.

2. Living up to brand promises and expectations is the evidence of a brand's integrity.

3. Under-promising and over-delivering delights customers, strengthening brand recall.

4. Great people and great experiences create winning brands.

5. It's not only what people *see* that counts. It's what they *believe* based on their actual or anticipated experiences.

6. Winning brands develop from the inside out.

7. Winning brands integrate market feedback into their planning and products.

8. Branding accelerates when business leaders pay attention to internal issues and communicate virally.

9. Following the "Seven I's of Accelerated Branding©", continuing brand efforts with a CQI (Continuous Quality Improvement) mindset, and recording results creates a dynamic book of brand wisdom.

10. Capturing brand wisdom and practicing it makes the brand come alive. (Don't leave your own book of brand wisdom on the shelf! Activate it!)

The Seven I's of Brand Acceleration©

The Seven I's of Brand Acceleration© — *Introspection, Inspiration, Innovation, Image development, Internal alignment, Inner resilience,* and *Integration* — are interlocking pathways to brand success. Together, they create a synergy that powerfully strengthens a brand from the inside out and helps build brand resilience. *Introspection* will help you see your brand more clearly. Exploring *inspiration* will help define what moves you and motivates leaders. A mindset of *innovation* will keep you focused on how to grow. *Image* encourages prime consumers to connect with you. *Internal alignment* will help ensure that what you do inside is a supportive match for the brand message you communicate externally. *Inner Resilience* will keep you focused on brand goals in every environment. And *Integration* efforts will help you pull together the many dynamic forces that influence a brand together.

Money alone does not create a powerful brand. Few businesses start out with the money they need to make a big market splash. Entrepreneurs struggle to maximize limited resources, while testing varied strategies for success. Working alongside business leaders, I've learned that it is the testing and validating process, then responding to market-based feedback, that helps speed a brand's success. I observed branding activities, analyzed brand experiences, diagnose "brand disorders," [1] captured information from consumers, and reflected on brand impact. As a result, I now share with you the most effective strategy for building a resilient, sustainable brand — integrated branding. Integrated branding strategy — fueled by the "Seven I's of Brand Acceleration" — works because it integrally links internal operations with external marketing efforts for the strongest possible impact. Think of it as building a strong, resilient mesh to support your brand through thick and thin.

Defining the Branding Process

A brand is a reputation based on thoughts, beliefs, and perceptions about companies and their products and services. Branding is the art of creating, building, or enhancing a positive image while raising awareness and preference for those products and services. Branding, like beliefs, is an "inside-out" process that far exceeds promoting recognition of an iconic design. Branding means creating sticky images and experiences that sharpen recall. Brand developers work to extend those images beyond simple recognition of a visual icon to lasting feelings and beliefs. And they design brands to evoke hopes, dreams, and expectations. The goal of branding is to trigger desired perceptions, thoughts, and buying patterns. And the ultimate goal of branding is to sell stuff.

Before you can sell, you need to understand the buyer's mindset and acknowledge that buying begins inside the head. The decision to buy into a brand premise or product, as well as how long it takes a buyer to decide to buy, is a reflection of the connection a brand makes with its customer. That connection depends on how accurately brand developers anticipated customer's concerns and tapped into their mental wiring. Brands are designed to create lingering experiences that activate a customer's senses through words such as: see, look, notice (visual words); listen, hear, tune in (auditory words); and feel, touch, experience (kinesthetic words).

---

[1] Brand disorder is the term I use to refer to a lack of hypothesis testing, validation, internal alignment, and integration, and/or disconnect between a brand's intent and the way it is perceived by consumers.

The key is to learn how people process language and speak to them in language that makes it more likely that they will notice and process words or images you present. Brand connections accelerate when branders link themselves to customers with words or experiences that match a customer's own neural set up.

Branding experts work to lure consumers, one delicious sensory bite at a time, with the goal of leaving a lingering taste that entices consumers to want more of the same. (Can you tell I recall the sense of taste?) Branding is mostly about understanding what motivates and sticks in the minds of consumers, then getting and staying inside those consumer minds. Before you can reside in someone else's mind, you need to look inside your own mind and brand premise. Here's how to speed up the process.

Brand Accelerator #1
INTROSPECTION

"I shut my eyes in order that I may see."
- Eugène Henri Paul Gauguin

Post-impressionist artist Eugène Henri Paul Gauguin was a celebrated painter, sculptor, print-maker, ceramist, and writer of the late 1800s. A native of France, Gauguin's bold expressionistic works gave deep meaning to his art and subjects. Gauguin's work synthesized the outward appearance of natural forms with his feelings about his subjects, through use of aesthetic elements of line, color, and form.

Brand artists also work to synthesize features: the outward appearance of products and services, along with the sensory experience buyers get from those products and services, and the brand's functional positioning in the minds of consumers, as compared to other choices in the market.

Understanding the assumptions, thoughts, perceptions, and dynamic beliefs that shape your brand will help you unlock your brand's potential. Start by looking inside your brand at foundational elements — business goals, hopes, dreams, beliefs, expectations, and resources. Internal scrutiny will help you break through thought, belief, perceptual, and resource barriers that limit your thinking and get in the way of your success. When you clarify your brand goals (intentions) and root your efforts in customer-centric business values — you make the brand more specific and relevant to your market. Exploring the inner meaning of your brand by asking the right questions — *What meaning do I make of my brand? What meaning will customers make of it?* — will guide you to branding actions that will propel you forward faster.

Brand Identity Exercise
IDENTIFYING THE REAL YOU

This exercise will help you create a powerful brand identity by helping you understand your own beliefs, perceptions, and perspective about your brand. By taking time to answer a series of questions about your business, you can uncover important information to use in your brand messages. Take a moment to consider the following questions. Your answers will provide your mind with a framework to guide the complex process of brand decision-making:

- *What brands do you admire? Why? Which brands don't you like? Why?*
- *Which of your competitors do you admire? Why?*
- *Which competitors don't you like? Why?*
- *Who are you as a brand? What do you do?*
- *What is your area of expertise or special differentiator?*
- *What makes you an expert in your field? Why should you be trusted?*
- *What kind of an image do you want to present to the world?*
- *What kind of clients/customers do you serve?*
- *Who are your target customers? Whom else do you want to reach?*
- *What do your customers want from you? How do you know?*
- *What does your own brand represent to you? To others? Who says so?*

- *What does your brand deliver to customers? To the community? To the world?*
- *How does your brand accomplish that?*
- *What is your geographic reach?*
- *What do you want people to believe about you (your business)? Where is the evidence?*
- *What do you want people to experience through your products/services?*
- *What do you want people to say about what they experience? Is it true? Can they say it now?*

If the answers people give mirror what you want them to believe, then your branding effort is on track.

The Impact of Beliefs

Brands are built on beliefs. Beliefs must be rooted in truth to be sustainable. Here are five helpful truths about brand management to get you started.

1. Innovation gets you first to market and keeps you ahead of the curve.
2. Provocative imagery captures and sustains attention.
3. Concrete differentiators articulate value.
4. Market responses based on customer trials, experience, and testimonials deliver important feedback about your brand.
5. Attention to customer feedback keeps a brand vital.

To move your brand forward, consider your beliefs about your brand.

1. *What holds you back?*
2. *What gets in the way of your brand identity, success, or strength?*
3. *What story are you telling yourself? Is it True?*

LIMITING BELIEFS Are you saying or believing the following?	BRAND EMPOWERMENT BELIEFS *Would this belief empower and help you move forward? Check your beliefs! Choose the belief that propels you forward.*
With the current economy, now is not a good time to market my brand.	*Now is the perfect time to test my brand. With so many other brands holding back, I can stand out and capture attention better than in a strong market.*
I don't have the money.	*I can allocate the money if I budget differently, or I can raise the money I need.*
People won't buy it.	*I will give people a good reason to buy now.*
We already have done all we can.	*If I evaluate the market, I might find other opportunities or areas I haven't explored that could make a greater impact.*
I'll think about it later.	*I am setting aside time now to learn what is needed to resolve my brand worries.*
I am too busy.	*I can work more effectively if I manage my time and resources or outsource my branding needs.*
We have too much stock on the shelves now so we don't have to brand.	*Marketing our brand will help us move stock out of the warehouse.*
I'll make do with what I have going now.	*I can create significant breakthrough outcomes if I learn how.*

I don't know how to effect a brand change.	*I will learn how by asking for help, researching strategies, finding new resources, and practicing new techniques.*
I am afraid to change my brand because I could end up worse off.	*People will respond to a brand that responds to them. If I change responsively and responsibly, people will respond in kind.*
People won't "get" what I am trying to do.	*I will learn to communicate more effectively in different ways.*
It will cost too much.	*I can ramp up over time.*
I already know everything I need to do, but the timing is just not right.	*I can make it work as long as I stay in continuous learning mode and learn how to adjust to variations in the market, and/or company requirements*

Shaping Your Brand Story

Your brand story, or meaning, is conveyed in many ways.

1. **Brand Message.** *What does your brand say or show to others? What does your brand message promise your customers?*

2. **Brand Positioning.** *How do you position your brand in the minds of customers by comparison to other products and services in the market? Are you setting expectations for the luxury or economy model? The fantastic experience or the generic supplier? The instant gratifier or the long-term satisfier? Are you trying to capture the market based on your reputation for quality, innovation, cost, or service?* After you choose the position you want to occupy, you can set criteria that will help you measure when you get there — and based on your criteria for success, and resources — you can work up an integrated branding plan.

3. **Brand Values.** *What do you / your company / your investors believe is important? How do those values mesh?* Without integrity, branding doesn't work. Make sure that your brand is a strong reflection of your company values and vice versa.

4. **Brand Ethics.** *Do you do conduct your business in a way that honors your brand promise? Are you sure? Where is your evidence?* A brand's reputation is linked to company ethics.

5. You can start a brand with words and messages, but you (and your products!) must walk the talk to gain a sustainable market hold.

6. **Brand Promise.** *Do you, your company, products, and services live up to the expectations you set?* Hold everyone in your organization accountable for walking the talk! Those who do will serve as terrific brand ambassadors. Those who don't will undermine your brand.

7. **Brand Evidence.** *What evidence tells consumers that your story is true?* Add credibility-building stories, testimonials, and references. Use keyword-rich articles on Internet sites to link your brand evidence with prospect queries.

8. **Brand Profitability.** *Does your brand work for you? Is it sustainable in the market?* You must continually tie brand efforts to the business needs and goals. Measure your brand's effectiveness using customer and prospect surveys (easier than ever with Internet-based tools), brand expansion, and the ability to extend your brand to new and different product lines. Be sure to integrate business values and ethics with bottom-line accounts management. Brands must be relevant to consumer needs; relevant brands succeed. Those that don't probably didn't do due diligence.

Your brand story defines the expected experience with your brand; conversely, that experience validates (or not) the meaning of your brand. Remember also that customers tell their own story. It's your job as a brand marketer to make sure they match. Your customers are your best brand resources. Teach them, through great experiences and brand messages, how to share the word about your brand.

Challenging Brand Assumptions

The exercises below offer you a chance to test your brand premise and challenge your assumptions. Taking the brand challenge is important because the main reason brands flop is that brand developers skip this critical aspect of due diligence. They don't ask the right questions, gather enough information, or test their business assumptions before rushing whole hog to market.

Are your brand assumptions working for you? *Do you and others get exactly what you want and expect from your brand?* Most brands (and businesses) are won or lost on assumptions. Test your assumptions by asking questions and setting criteria for good brand decisions. Make sure the answers reflect the intention for your brand, and verify that your brand promise connects with your business intentions and values, as well as with those of targeted consumers. How strong is your brand? *Can a consumer rely on your brand promise 100% of the time?* As you explore your brand, also consider that brands are made of two things: your concepts and the consumers' perception of your concepts.

Your goal (should you choose to accept this challenge!) is to create a brand that relates well to its intended consumers. Start by learning how people in your market think and buy, then challenge your assumptions. To see your brand from the inside out, get introspective. Look inside, at your own brand assumptions. *What do you think your brand stands for? What story does your brand tell? What expectations does it set about your products and services? What do your customers say about your brand now? What do you want them to say? How can you get them to say it? What could be affecting your brand? What else might be important to consumers?*

How can you confirm and/or measure that? What if your assumptions are wrong?

Challenge Questions

1. *What are you trying to achieve? How are you measuring up so far?*
2. *What do you want instead of what you've got now? What can you do differently to get that?*
3. *What product, service, and people attributes would help your brand become more resilient and sustainable, able to bounce back despite challenging circumstances?*
4. *What gives this brand its power?*
5. *What do you see when you look at your brand?*
6. *What do you hear people saying about your brand or products/services?*
7. *What do you and others feel about your brand?*
8. *What expectations does your brand create?*
9. *What patterns, e.g., reactions, buying behavior, expectations, proof, emerge in relation to your brand?*
10. *What steps would help you improve your brand message?*

You will make better branding decisions, and become better at forecasting results, when you regularly assess your assumptions and efforts. Use diagnostic tools, such as feedback from focus groups and surveys, marketing research, and accounting and statistical analysis to gain insight to your brand effort impact. Using tools to measure the gaps between targeted and actual results helps you build a stronger, more market-responsive brand. Testing your assumptions helps you develop more reliable market intelligence, which in turn will help you adjust your branding efforts in the right places at the right times.[2]

Introspection Exercise
BRAND GOALS

The *Brand Accelerator Assessment© Worksheet* below will help you understand what your own thoughts, feelings, and experiences with your brand mean to you and the world around you. You can

---

[2] Donna Anselmo, *Marketing Demystified,* McGraw-Hill 2010, Principles of Branding, page 29.

analyze and better understand your brand when you shut out extraneous market noise, such as worries about competition and demands that don't fit your brand personality. For example, many branding efforts succeed better in niche markets, and the smaller the better. Choosing a niche allows you to concentrate your resources for better impact than a scattershot approach at a mass market. Learn the best fit between your brand intentions and your most likely (and most desired) customers. You probably don't have the resources to market (or deliver) to the world at large, so you may want to design your brand message for the niche most likely to respond.

BOLD MARKETING SOLUTIONS, INC. BRAND ACCELERATOR ASSESSMENT©	
RATE YOUR BRAND 1 – Got it Covered 2 – Working on It, But Need Help 3 - Haven't Addressed It Yet	BRAND ACCELERATORS
	Clarity of Purpose / Mission
	Recognizable as an Entity
	Talked About
	Know Where Brand Belongs / Clear on Positioning
	Know Where Brand is Going (Vision of the Future)
	Connecting with People / Buyers / Influencers
	Targeting Breakthrough Outcomes
	Able to Plan Effectively for Ongoing Success
	Able to Identify Appropriate Next Steps and Stay on Goal
	Able to Adapt as Needed – (What Do You Do When Your Brand Effort is Off Goal?)

	Learn to Identify Limiting Beliefs, Self-Defeating Brand Choices, and Business Behaviors
	Able to Step Out of Brand Assumptions to See How Customers, Employees, and Prospects Really See Your Brand
	Change Limiting Beliefs, Perceptions, Approaches and Patterns of Business to Create Stronger Brand Success and Stronger Teams
	Reach Brand Maturity by Staying Aware of Inner and Outer Brand Obstacles
	Identify and Eliminate Self-Defeating Brand Characteristics, Business Behaviors, and Choices That Get in the Way of Success
	Focus on What is In Your Control and Influence
	Take Action to Ensure Quality / Value. (Use Continuous Quality Improvement Method: Plan, Do, Check, Act)
	Connect Strongly with Customers
	Create Strong Value for Customers and/or the World
	Create Sustainable Business Branding Model

Now review your numbers. Congratulate yourself for all of your "1" ratings. Ask yourself what resources and special help you need to move your "2" ratings to a number "1" slot. Stay in continuous learning mode to build your skills and resources. Ask yourself why you have not yet made progress in the areas you have rating a "3". Make a plan with an action timeline for launching brand accelerators and achieving milestones.

Brand Accelerator #2
INSPIRATION

Sustainable brands offer great experiences. Do you envision a bigger, brighter future where your brand becomes synonymous with a great experience? Where does that vision come from?

Who or what inspires you has the power to propel you forward. Fuel your branding effort by transforming brand stressors into brand energy. Rather than worry over your competition, use today's brand leaders as your inspiration. The success of brand icons such as Coca Cola, IBM, Arm & Hammer, Apple, Google, Twitter, and McDonald's pushes you to look past what those brands have achieved to what you can do to achieve success on a grand scale, or even in your own small region. There's a lot to be said for a simple business mode. Look inside your own brand to identify what you can do differently to reach your branding goals. Explore what inspires you. Encourage yourself (or your team if you have one) to have fun and think even zany thoughts. Inspiration can fuel creativity.

When seeking inspiration, ask questions and prime your mind to answer. Ask your questions out loud, so your brain can hear and work on them. Don't force the answers. Let your thoughts percolate for a bit. Define criteria for ideas that will help you enhance your brand. *What would a good idea be like?* When you get answers, decide how to test them.

How do you tell the world about your brand? Follow the people and brands you are interested in, inspired by, or would like to model on Twitter. Watch how they move and dissect how they do it. Move yourself forward by following models proven to work. Learn from great brands, and model them. (You might even find some brand leaders following you back.)

Inspiration Exercise

Step into the genius of a brand you admire. Consider your brand through that brand developer's eyes.

1. *Which brands do you admire? Why?*
2. *How would that inspirational role model see your situation?*
3. *What would (s)he do or advise?*
4. *Mentally step into that model's shoes. Tell that model your concern, problem.*
5. *State the outcome you want instead of the problem or indecision you have.*
6.
7. *Listen in your mind. What would that person or branding expert say?*

Brand Accelerator #3
INNOVATION

Innovative brands generate ideas, products, experiences, and environments that shift beliefs, perceptions, thoughts, and expectations to new levels. Innovators step up themselves and empower themselves to challenge the status quo about what their brand communicates. *What does your brand communicate? Suppose you are wrong? What if everything you did failed? What would you do next?* (The answer is **NOT** pack up and go home. The answer is *INNOVATE!*)

The power to innovate lies in one's permission to change the rules. Eliminate recriminations and fear of failure. Run "what if" scenarios through your mind and your team's collective minds, as if you were a computer with a special application that could provide an array of novel answers on command. Give yourself the freedom to come up with a different shaped wheel, or even better, discard the wheel shape entirely and reveal a product or process enhancement that breaks entirely new ground. Who thought adding hot purple, green, orange, and blue to desktop computers would send sales skyrocketing? Not the people who approached computers only through the lens of computing. It took looking at computers in a new way. Apple broke the rules, and they learned that computers didn't have to look serious to be serious players. Computers needed to take on a personality that matched that of their prospective owners. Suddenly, computer geeks could fulfill their fantasy to be cutting edge, fashionable, and color coordinated, too.

Apple is synonymous with innovation because Steve Jobs pressed the essence of a product and looked for compelling new ways to shift a user's experience and pleasure. Apple also built its brand on reliability. What message does this innovative company inspire in you? Apple is still innovating because that's what people have come to expect, and will continue to expect, even in the post-Steve Jobs era.

How do you innovate? Focus on building a free, collaborative, and creative environment. Set the expectation that your products (and brand message) must end up 100% reliable and meet or exceed all customer expectations. Open lines of communication inside your company. Letting information flow both ways – inside out and outside in — will help you stay in touch with your audience.

Another path to innovation and brand acceleration is to shift your perspective. Imagine that your market is a maze and you have to sort your way through. You might try going left or right a few times, and tracking your turns to see your way to the end goal and open territory beyond. How else could you see your way out? Imagine that you can float above the maze and see your customers from an aerial view that would give you added perspective. With the clarity of a new vantage point, you could find the shortest pathway more quickly. While a map or geo-positioning tool might show you a route from Point A to Point B, you still may find that it is not the quickest route. Your map might not account for traffic, construction, or weather conditions, which change all the time. An aerial view would help you incorporate everything else you know about what is appropriate to your own situation. In essence, it would speed up your decision making and help you choose the right strategy.

Likewise, incorporating other perspectives is one strategy you can use to promote brand innovation.

Step outside the box by giving yourself permission to think differently and shift your perspective. *What can you see on the horizon that isn't apparent on first look? Gaze through the haze to see what forms you make out. What do you predict consumers will respond to?* Test your predictions by toeing into the market and evaluating your effort before putting all your eggs in the basket.

Shifting Perspective
To understand potential consequences and see the big picture, try shifting perspective. Start by setting your intention. *What are you hoping to achieve? What will it look like, feel like, and sound like when you get there?*

Here are some perspective-shifting strategies. Imagine you are looking at your options from present and future vantage points:
1. *How would your answers be different based on your market timing?*
2. *What would you say based on your past experience?*
3. *What change would you love to make if you knew how?*
4. *What result would you love to get if you knew how?*
5. *Put yourself in your customers' shoes. How would they view your brand now?*
6. *What factors influence your brand now?*
7. *What might influence your brand in the future?*
8. *How might you portray your brand differently in the future?*
9. *How will customers view it in the future (or if you added a new service, product, or logo)?*

Brand Accelerator #4
INTERNAL ALIGNMENT

While thinking about perspective, consider how your brand reflects the perspective of your employees and other stakeholders, such as investors, vendors, and consumers. What stories are your employees telling themselves, each other, and the world outside your headquarters about you? What could they be saying in the future?

1. *If you are an employee of the future, what are you looking for? What culture would make you think yours is the greatest company going?*
2. *If you are a customer of the future, what would you look for? What would you expect this company to provide for you?*

Sustainable brands align their mission, vision, core values, and culture with their message. They communicate well and often with their constituents (employees, customers, prospects, and stakeholders). Core values are the standards that are important enough to serve as the governing anchors for a company. They create the foundation for how you conduct your life and work. They provide constancy for brand choices and an effective anchor for decisions.

Objectives of Internal Branding
1. *Connect employees to your brand*
2. *Cultivate passionate, highly-engaged employees*
3. *Create a seamless, differentiated experience for your target audiences*
4. *Be more competitive in the market*

Brand Value Alignment Exercise
Make a circle on a sheet of paper and divide it into slices, like a pie. Inside each slice, write one of your personal core values. Have your leadership team and colleagues do the same.

Are your personal values (what is most important to you) reflected in what you promote about your brand? Does your brand reliably honor those values in terms of products, service, and outcomes?
Note: When doing this exercise with colleagues, discuss this and explore how to bring personal values in line with leadership values and brand messages and product development.

Next, imagine you are stepping inside one of those values and wrap yourself in the sense of it.

Then, from the perspective of that value:
• *State the message that value would send you about your brand.*
• *Visualize what that message outcome or action would look like, feel like, and sound like from your brand.*
• *Send a message to yourself from that value about your brand. What would you say?*
• *Consider the insight you gain.*

Brand Accelerator #5
IMAGE

Helpful Questions for Shaping Your Brand Message
Use the questions below as a guide to help you identify the most important elements of your brand message. They will guide you to choose powerful words that will connect with your target prospects.

- *What does your brand look like, sound like, and feel like to your customers inside their minds and bodies? What physical reactions can you predict?*
- *Will they see a logo (a graphic icon) or a logotype (font) that attracts them? What will it tell them about you?*
- *Does your logo look professional? Could it use a facelift?*
- *What do people see when they read your ads, or visit your store, office, or website?*
- *Do your ads feature actual products or fantasies?*
- *Do you need to change your ads? If so, what do you think would be helpful?*
- *What words and images do people see when they look on your shelves or at your building?*
- *What do they see when you or your sales team visit them? What image do you project? Do they see suits and ties, classic business attire, branded shirts? What does this tell them?*

- *What words, images, and feelings do they hear when listening to a commercial, radio announcement, employee, friend, or someone else about you?*
- *What do they sense, touch, feel, or experience when they get to know you or your products and services?*

Remember it's not about you. Your message first needs to be about what the customer thinks and experiences. Your message needs to make your customers feel and believe that your brand is *the only one* that can give them *the only product or service they want.* This is the process that marketers call product or service *differentiation.*

For the most part, customers don't care much about your company's capabilities sheet or your product ingredients. They want to know what you and your products can *do* for them. Then do what you say you are going to do. That is the ultimate test of brand image. When your image matches your brand promise, your brand value expands.

Brand Accelerator #6
INNER RESILIENCE

Brand Resilience — *n.* 1. The power to create a sustainable, recognizable brand presence, achieve consistent positive regard, and elicit desired responses to products and services from customers, employees, brand ambassadors, investors, and the world beyond 2. The ability to maintain integrity while creating conscious, flexible goal-oriented strategies, regardless of the environment.

Inner Resilience — *n.* The state of inner well-being that enables us to act both on instinct and reliable information because we have replaced fear of failure with our belief in ourselves, our confidence to overcome obstacles, our passion for our life, products, and brand, and our commitment to action. **Outcome:** We reach our goals and have learned how to flex and how to create and hold gains.

Building a Resilient Brand

Building a resilient brand is like installing a safety net so your brand will bounce back, even from crisis situations. Resilient brands rely on resilient people inside the organization. Build a culture of resilient people — people who stay focused and don't flap up and down based on failure, rejection of an idea, criticism, or disappointment —and you will build a resilient brand.

People who take 100% responsibility for brand successes and failures alike build resilient brands. Regardless of success or failure they press forward to identify breakthrough goals, prepare action plans, and determine realistic next steps. Resilient brands are adaptable because they move forward based on verifiable information. They learn what is needed to reach breakthrough goals, and they stay in the game – despite disappointments – to build endurance. They learn to accept failure as a learning experience. By trial and error or modeling, they learn to do the right things right. In doing so, they gain consumer (and board) confidence based on continuous learning and feedback. The resilient brand becomes recognized for success after success.

The Link between Inner Resilience and Branding

Every brand was conceived in the mind of a person or group of people. So, to move brands forward, we have to move people forward to create the kind of momentum that pushes brands forward. When individuals shift their inner thinking, beliefs, and perceptions into a resilient mode built on belief in themselves, they also build their judgment, decision-making, and ability to recover *no matter what*. As a result, they worry less and are less easily distracted. They focus more and act more. Brands are built on action.

What does that mean for you as a brand marketer? You can learn to model peak performance[3] behaviors and overcome negative thinking, fear of making the wrong choice, etc. You can demonstrate a resilient mindset so that your team can adopt it too, and work

---

[3] Email donna@boldmarketingsolutions.com for a free peak performance self-evaluation.

effectively to promote your brand. By adopting the behaviors and mindset of resilient performers and applying that thinking behavior and learning from personal resilience to branding, you will be better able to:

1. Assess where you are today against where you want to be.
2. Identify the best ways to close the gap.
3. Learn what you need to learn.
4. Figure out what resources you need.
5. Draw up your plan.
6. Act on your plan.

Brand Accelerator #7
INTEGRATION

It is critical to integrate your internal mission, operations, and culture with sales and external operations. Strategic, integrated multi-modal communication will strengthen brand connections. Add credibility-building videos, video testimonials, references, word of mouth advertising, and articles to your marketing mix. Place key word rich-phrases and articles on your website and others (especially if the journalists don't respond) and communicate across media channels (TV, radio, newspapers, magazines, web blogs, websites, cross-links, etc.) to reinforce your presence.

Successful branders don't live inside a bubble; they reach out, engage with consumers, and learn as much as possible about their markets. I would be remiss not to mention market research as important, even in this chapter on brand acceleration. Knowing your market is essential to building a relevant brand. Successful branding agents rotate and twist the bubble, testing market opportunities until they find or create opportunities that are a good fit for the brand story, or they take the story to a new and more exciting level.

Become an expert in mindfulness. Study industry needs and how other companies are meeting them. *What do you know about the needs of your market? What do you know about the direction and goals of your competitors?* When market factors change, a brand doesn't need to change, but its approach to the market may need alteration. Stay market mindful and adjust image and branding campaigns accordingly. (Other chapters in this book address marketing tactics.) Whatever brand image or position you choose, measure your effectiveness continually. Stay tuned to how and where you appear in search engines. Measure Internet mentions and customer preferences. Stay abreast of the latest social networking tools to connect with your target markets. Build a reputation for giving your customers what they need.

Acceleration Tips

* Look inside your brand. Check beliefs (internal and external) and act on them.
* Know your audience.
* Conduct research. Gather the facts about your market.
* Focus on actions that support the brand position you choose.
* Build products and brand messaging that are relevant to and mindful of your audience.
* Innovate to stay relevant.
* Watch the market and observe people and brands that inspire you.
* Build and protect your brand image by delivering on your promises.
* Enhance your persona as an expert or preferred provider in your field.
* Communicate a clear message consistently in ways that stimulate visual, auditory, and kinesthetic channels.
* Give consumers special, positive, memorable experiences.
* Develop inner resilience for external impact.
* Integrate your internal mission, operations, and culture with sales and external operations.

Donna Anselmo is an award-winning communications expert, strategic business consultant, radio personality, founder of BOLD Marketing Solutions, Inc., and author of *Marketing Demystified,* a bestseller published by McGraw-Hill in 2010. Tapped as an expert by media and professional organizations, Donna has been quoted in *Newsday, Long Island Business News,* and various print and broadcast media including CBS, News 12, WMEL, and Jobline on topics relating to the economy, leadership, change management, business, legislation, injury prevention, and health policy, among other subjects.

Donna is best known for her ability to translate complex information into user-friendly messaging. As a marketing communicator, she is lauded for brand messaging strategies that move people to desired action and promote brand recall. Over her career, Donna has delivered the full range of integrated business services — strategic plans, marketing, public relations, operations, training, brand design and graphic design — to a diverse cross-industry clientele in sectors including banking, finance, education, healthcare, staffing, technology, manufacturing, and non-profit, among others.

Passionate about helping people and companies achieve personal and business breakthroughs, Donna teaches powerful strategies that build the inner resources, resilience, leadership, creativity, planning, and relationships that lead to success. With international reach, Donna has empowered thousands through her book, weekly AM radio broadcasts, leadership coaching, strategic consulting, speaking engagements, and informative articles.

Follow Donna on Facebook at **Donna.Anselmo** or Twitter at **@DonnaAnselmo**.

Visit **BoldMarketingSolutions.com** for relevant, ongoing insight, strategies, tips, and tools for your success.

Media Magic

Supplemental Chapter
5
The World's Greatest Business Card
by Keith Leon

The following is an excerpt from Keith Leon's book, *The Bake Your Book Program; How to finish your book fast and serve it up HOT!* co-written with Maribel Jimenez.

Let's Get Cookin'

How many times have you heard someone say, "Someday, I'm going to write a book," or "If I just had the time, I'd write a book, too," or "I just know I have a book inside of me that needs to come out." Perhaps you've even made one of these statements yourself. You're about to change that story.

Did you know 81% of Americans say they want to write a book? The truth is anyone can write a book, but we've been told only 1% of people who say they want to actually will. Only 1% of people will do anything they say they want to do. It's a startling statistic, but it's true. We have a personal mission to change this statistic.

This book will show you the tools and format that were used to create the best-selling book, *Who Do You Think You Are?* among other successful books. With these tips, you can create the book you always wanted to write. We'll show you ways to get support to create your book with a community of others through the *Bake Your Book* Mentoring Program to make it a reality.

It's far more important to get your message out to the world than it is to produce the perfect masterpiece many people aspire to create. There is really no such thing as the perfect book. Every author we know could pick up their book right now and show you the things they wish they could have fixed or changed before going to print. It's this type of thinking that stops so many people from ever calling their book "done" and getting it out to people who really need to read it.

Your message is important. People need the information you have been keeping to yourself all this time. Even if you think what you know isn't unique, we guarantee there is someone out there who doesn't know it, and wants to.

The 5 Advantages of Being a Published Author

Let's take a look at just some of the benefits you gain by being a published author.

1. Credibility – By becoming a published author in an area you are familiar, you position yourself as an expert in your field. You've taken the time to provide valuable information on a topic from which others could benefit, so you become a resource.

Having credibility means you gain belief by others in your area of expertise that could otherwise take years to build.

2. Respect – You are the person who actually *DID* write a book, instead of the one who said you would and never did. You have now identified yourself as a *doer* instead of a *talker* or a *dreamer*.

A level of respect is gained by doing something others only dream of doing. As mentioned earlier in this book, it has been said that only 1% of those who say they want to write a book, actually do.

3. Clients – More people will want to work with you than ever before. Being an expert in your field opens up many more windows of opportunity to get your name out to potential clients, and will add credibility when you're a guest on radio shows, television programs, Webinars and tele-seminars.

The quality of your clients will improve because you've positioned yourself as an expert in your field, allowing you to charge more for your work. As an expert, your clients will treat you as a serious professional and no longer attempt to get discounts for your valuable time and services.

With a book, your message reaches more people than you could possibly talk to one at a time. Potential clients have an opportunity to get to know you and what you're about, and decide that they want to learn more from you, all before they've even met you.

4. Raving Fans – There's nothing more satisfying than having someone in front of you, sharing how your book touched their life, or receiving an email or letter from a raving fan. Your book will help someone get to where they always wanted to be and they'll be grateful to you.

5. Testimonials – Once you receive these stories from people whose lives you've helped change for the better, you will have testimonials for your website, articles, proposals, bio, and for your next book. Anytime a person shares how you've helped them, ask them to put it in writing, so you can share his inspiring story with others. Everyone wins. It's a win for the author, the person giving the testimonial, and for the reader.

Your Book Is Now Your Business Card

In the past, people would meet at a dinner or event to connect. One would ask the other for a business card, and the next time they needed the service of the person they'd met, they'd pull out the card and call. This was a way of doing business, and it worked. In the present day of cell phones, iPhones, Blackberries, Blueberries, and all kinds of phone berries, this old-school way of doing business no longer works. Business cards are too easy to lose in the shuffle of a busy day.

Many of you spend piles of money going to so-called "networking events" hoping to meet potential clients who need the service you offer. Or perhaps, you hope to meet other like-minded people with whom to collaborate on future projects. You spend hours listening to speakers, missing sleep, and rushing through meals, all to go home with a stack of business cards. How many of those business cards do you follow up on? We have a personal rule: Don't take anyone's card unless you're willing to follow up as soon as you return home, even if it's in the middle of the night after a 3-day event. Even if you personally follow up on every card you take, you rarely, if ever, hear back from the person you reached out to after the event was over.

Most men will throw the stack of cards in the trash as soon as they get home and unpack. Some women are nice enough to put them into a nice stack and wrap a rubber band around them. They'll hold onto this rubber-banded stack of cards until the next time they clean out their desks and, at that point, the cards go right into the circular file also known as a trash can. It seems harsh, but think about how many times you have actually heard from anyone you handed one of your cards to.

Let's face it. Almost all business cards look the same. Most are the same shape, size, thickness and colors. Some may have a picture of the person who gave you the card, which is a step in the right direction, but it's not enough to keep you from tossing the card in the waste basket the next chance you get.

When we hand someone a copy of our book, they feel honored. Most of the time the person we give the book to will ask us to sign it. If he is a reader, he'll go home and read the book, personally getting to know us and our work in the world. If he isn't really a reader, he'll go home and set the book down somewhere or put it on his bookshelf. Then, the next reader who comes along will say, "Hey, what's this book?' and before you know it, he's reading the book and becoming a fan of ours.

Here's how you can change the typical scenario into a better one. Instead of tossing your card as soon as he gets home, he now has something from you that tells him all about you and lets him get to know you personally. He may share what he's learned about you with his friends and family. The worst case scenario is he'll give the book to someone whom he cares about with his highest recommendation, and you end up with yet another raving fan.

Your book is your card, which sets you apart from your competition and positions you as an expert. We believe there is enough recognition for everyone, so we don't play the competition game. Instead we do things that set us apart from others who do similar work. We like to be the very best at what we do, and are big into providing value for our customers. It's better to over-deliver than to under-deliver.

So, instead of handing out a card, hand out your book. Do you give a book to everyone? No. Instead, you can use a series of questions to identify your perfect clients. If, after answering these questions, you think the person is a match for your services, then hand her a copy of your book.

Additionally, you can carry an extra copy to give to a person who appears to be in the perfect place to use the book's content to uplift his situation. He may not be the best candidate to become a client, but could use the information or inspiration. You will know when to share your book with a person who needs it. He'll be grateful to receive it, and you'll likely hear a follow-up story about how the book came at just the perfect time for him.

 **Keith Leon** is a multiple best-selling author, publisher, book mentor, and is well known as, "The Book Guy." With his wife, Maura, Keith co-authored the book, *The Seven Steps to Successful Relationships*, acclaimed by best-selling authors, John Gray and Terry Cole-Whittaker, and Keith authored the best-selling book, *Who Do You Think You Are? Discover the Purpose of Your Life*, with a foreword by Chicken Soup for The Soul's Jack Canfield.

Keith's writing has also been featured in Warren Henningsen's *If I Can You Can*, Jennifer McLean's *The Big Book of You*, Justin Sachs' *The Power of Persistence*, Ron Prasad's *Welcome To Your Life*, Anton Uhl's, *Feeding Body, Mind and Soul*, Bardi Toto's, *Thinking Upside Down Living Rightside Up*, Keith Leon and Maribel Jimenez', *The Bake Your Book Program, How to Finish Your Book Fast* and *Serve it Up HOT*, and many other books, including his latest bestseller, *YOU Make a Difference: 50 Heart-Centered Entrepreneurs Share Their Stories of Inspiration and Transformation*.

Keith has appeared on popular radio and television broadcasts, including "The Rolonda Watts Show" and "The John Kerwin Show," and his work has been covered by LA Weekly, The Valley Reporter, The Minneapolis-St. Paul Star Tribune, and The Maryland Herald-Mail, The Huffington Post, and Succeed Magazine just to name a few.

As a professional speaker, life and relationship mentor, and a developer and facilitator of transformational seminars, Keith is a recognized expert at building relationships that work. He has spoken at events that included Jack Canfield, Dr. John Demartini, Lee Brower, Christine Comaford-Lynch, Joel Bauer, Armand Morin, Paul Martinelli, Barbara De Angelis, Dr. John Gray, Dr. Michael Beckwith, Alex Mandossian, T. Harv Eker, Adam Markel, and Marianne Williamson.

Keith's list of clients include: Walt Disney Company, Universal Studios Hollywood, Warner Bros., Peak Potentials Training, New Regency Productions, 20th Century Fox, Bijan Fragrances, County of Los Angeles, Los Angeles Times, Microsoft, Mobil Oil, XEROX, NBC, CNBC, KNBC, MSNBC, CBS Press and Publicity, PBS, Fox Broadcasting, Fox Health Network, British Broadcasting Corporation, Greystone Communications, Image Associates, MEDIALINK, On the Scene Productions, Orbis Broadcast Group, West Glen Communications, John Rosas Productions, Visual Frontier, CF Entertainment, Weller-Grossman Productions, The Ronn Lucas Show, AMGEN, Bender Helper IMPACT, Fleishman-Hilliard Company, Golin/Harris Communications, Hill & Knowlton,

Ketchum Public Relations, Sitrick & Company, Meals on Wheels, Special Olympics, The Century Council, and The Agape International Spiritual Center.

Keith's passion is teaching people how to go from first thought to bestseller and how to manifest the life of their dreams. He does this through his personal mentoring, ghost writing services, home study course and offers any book service you need to get your book out to the world.

Find out more about Keith at **BabypiePublishing.com**

Do you have a book inside of you
that's begging to get OUT?

Would you like to grow your business
by up to 300%?

Now is the time to:

BAKE YOUR BOOK

Since you have this book in your hands, I know you're serious about getting your message out to the world. For this reason, I'm sharing my Bake Your Book step-by-step system with you for a **$600 savings** as my way of supporting your goal of creating what I call, *The World's Greatest Business Card.*

Get this program now, and you will:

- ✓ Finish writing your book this year!
- ✓ Learn THE most successful ways to market your book to grow your business
- ✓ Learn the exact steps needed to write and ask for a foreword and endorsement quotes
- ✓ Get FORMS, CHECKLISTS and word-for-word I have used to create a ton of bestselling books
- ✓ And much, much more!

You can access Bake Your Book Home Study Program details and savings here: www.BakeYourBookNow.com

Once you've clicked the buy now button, type in this special discount code: **MEDIA MAGIC** to receive your special price! See you soon, Keith

You're On Your Way!

"Oh the places you'll go...." - Dr. Seuss

Congratulations! You have now completed my *Media Magic* training and are ready to get your message out and grow your business. The skills you have learned throughout this course will enable you to develop and market your business efficiently and effectively.

Each of the Success Strategies in *Media Magic* has been designed to teach you specific skills and help you focus on creating and marketing the business you are meant to run.

- In "Visualize Your Future," you took the time to create a vision board - a key exercise that allows you to truly see what you want in your business and personal life.

- "What is Marketing?" provided a guide to developing a marketing plan specific to your business.

- Creating stories about you and events that have occurred in your life allows you to build connections with prospects and media contacts and make you 'real' in their eyes. "What's Your Story" walked you through writing these stories.

- In "Know Who You Are," I gave you the tools you need to write your 'Elevator Speech' or 'Conscious Calling' - a short, concise introduction to get your message across quickly and completely.

- "What's So Good About That?" reinforces the importance of always sharing your message in terms of benefits, rather than features. Your prospects want to know what your products and services can do for them, not just what they are.

- Another great way to build connections and help prospects and the media get to know you is creating your power bio. "Power in Your

- Bio" taught you the skills you need to pull your bio together with impact.

- "Stand Out From the Competition" is all about writing a press release. Getting a press release to the media is a highly effective way of getting your message out to a wide audience.

- After creating your power bio and press release, "Don't Miss the Boat" showed you how to put your press kit together to share your message and provide important marketing information to prospects and media contacts.

- Finally, you learned how to create a comprehensive media contact list and follow up with your contacts in "It's a Numbers Game."

You are now ready and armed with all of the tools and skills you need to make things happen for you and your business. Don't delay - get out there and make it happen today!

That's Easy!